Beyond the Flannel Board

Beyond the Flannel Board

STORY-RETELLING STRATEGIES
ACROSS THE CURRICULUM

M. SUSAN McWILLIAMS

Redleaf Press®
www.redleafpress.org
800-423-8309

Published by Redleaf Press
10 Yorkton Court
St. Paul, MN 55117
www.redleafpress.org

First edition 2017
Cover design by Tilt Design/Amy Fastenau
Cover photographs by iStock.com / Image Source (top), DIOMEDIA / Blend RF / Ariel Skelley (left), iStock.com / antares71 (center), iStock.com / Charles Schmidt (right)
Interior design by Mayfly Design
Typeset in the Minion, Whitney, Adoquin, and Sketchetik typefaces.
Interior photographs by the author
Printed in the United States of America
24 23 22 21 20 19 18 17   1 2 3 4 5 6 7 8

Library of Congress Cataloging-in-Publication Data
Names: McWilliams, M. Susan, author.
Title: Beyond the flannel board : story retelling strategies across the
   curriculum / M. Susan McWilliams.
Description: First edition. | St. Paul, MN : Redleaf Press, 2017. | Includes
   bibliographical references and index.
Identifiers: LCCN 2016047571 (print) | LCCN 2017007024 (ebook) | ISBN
   9781605544861 (paperback : alk. paper) | ISBN 9781605544878 (ebook)
Subjects: LCSH: Storytelling in education. | Storytelling ability in
   children. | Early childhood education. | BISAC: EDUCATION / Curricula. |
   EDUCATION / Teaching Methods & Materials / General. | EDUCATION /
   Preschool & Kindergarten. | EDUCATION / Teaching Methods & Materials /
   Reading & Phonics.
Classification: LCC LB1042 .M37 2017 (print) | LCC LB1042 (ebook) | DDC
   372.67/7—dc23
LC record available at https://lccn.loc.gov/2016047571

Printed on acid-free paper.

For Steve

Contents

Acknowledgments

Stories were always part of my life. I grew up in a family that at times gathered on the front porch of my great-grandfather's old home on steeping-hot Louisiana evenings. My brother and I played quietly in the grass while the old folks spun yarns and wove stories I'd never heard before or since. I remember the joy and comfort in knowing those family stories were my stories, in staying up late, being quiet with my brother (we were never quiet), hoping no one noticed that it was dark and well past bedtime, hoping no one noticed us at all—just listening and pretending to play and being invisible. It was pure magic.

Recently I realized that I'm still catching stories when they appear in my path. Although they are not old family stories, I'm still quietly making myself invisible and listening to stories. As a university supervisor in preschool and kindergarten classrooms, I listen to stories, hear interactions, observe story retelling, and realize that I am one lucky person. I often see young children visibly transformed at the mere presence of a book. I also realize that I have a lot of people to thank for helping me get to this place.

Dr. Sarah Edwards, Associate Dean David Conway, and Dean Nancy Edick were the first to see my proposal for this book. Their votes of confidence in granting a sabbatical leave propelled the project beyond an idea and into something tangible. Dr. Edwards's continued encouragement and support were pivotal when I returned to teaching while still engaged in writing.

The Omaha Family Literacy Partnership influenced this book greatly. This community-based organization promotes the joy of reading to young children and their families by hosting book distributions and author/illustrator events (made possible by the University of Nebraska–Omaha [UNO] College of Education, the UNO Office of Service Learning, First Book Foundation, Mrs. Carol Gendler, and others). This work informed my learning and my views on the creative potential held within a children's book.

I've always loved books published by Redleaf Press. I pored through their books at conferences, used them as textbooks in my courses, and referenced them in my writing. After this writing experience, I now know Redleaf Press as not only beautiful "on the cover" but just as fabulous inside. Laurie Herrmann patiently extracted the remaining chapters from me while I was teaching full-time. Danny Miller and Alyssa Lochner edited this book with expertise and respectfulness. Thank you, Alyssa and Danny.

I send special thanks to the extraordinary Isabel Baker, who writes about high-quality, worthwhile children's literature in her regular column "The Reading Chair" for NAEYC's *Young Children* journal. She visits Omaha annually (thanks to Jennifer Haggart's vision and resources) to update us on using high-quality children's literature with "rich words." Special thanks also to a great story-retelling team of early childhood master educators who graciously presented at an early literacy conference with me in fall of 2014: Jean Hearn, Loretta Novotny, Molly Moran, and Paula Szczepaniak.

This book could not have been possible without the help of many teachers, children, parents, and teacher candidates. Both preschool sites involved in this project provided me with access to observe and photograph teachers and children as they played with stories and conducted story enactments and retellings. They allowed me to place books, finger puppets, and other props into the classroom and to work with the children. I want to thank Jane Allen, director of Hamilton Heights Child Development Center (CDC), for providing me with access to her site. I greatly appreciate Eliza Reker, preschool teacher at Hamilton Heights CDC, as well as parents and children who participated in this project. Similarly, sincerest thanks go to Julie Oelke, District 66 Early Childhood Center (ECC) program director, and to Carly Mathews, director of Oakdale ECC, for providing me with site access. I appreciate Oakdale ECC parents and children who participated in the project. Warmest thanks go to Oakdale ECC educators who gave me permission to become their "very own paparazzi" in their classrooms: Nicole Borchardt, Jacquelyn Harper, Stacey Hussey, Kathy Holdsworth, Carly Mathews, Cecilia Q. Petersson, Courtney Sprague, and Kasey Wurst. Lastly, I thank the following UNO teacher candidates for permission to use photographs of their work: Dawn Adams, Samantha Boyle, Melinda Brewer, Brennan Chandler, Bailey B. Corcoran, Alyssa Dail, Linzee Gammell, Rebecca Hansen, Brittan Haynes, Abigail Jorgensen, Alexis Labenz, Claudia Magana-Magana, Sarah Miller, Shelby Soukup, Amber Stark, Keli O'Brien, Whitney Taylor, and Tiana Wilson.

Finally, I end with thanking my family. Bill and Billy Lewis raised me on family stories and silly poems and reading aloud before I learned to read—at about the same time that Dolores Durkin was gathering data for her first-grade studies—amazing parents! I thank my dear husband, Steve, who, as a result of this project, is now a great cook and an ace at housecleaning. He cheered me on throughout and remains a very patient person to this day. Thanks to Sarah, John, and Maureen McWilliams for their listening when I'd share project thoughts for the trillionth time. Last but not least, I am blessed with a precious grandchild, Maggie, who was between the ages of three and five when I wrote this book. I had an incredible view of the world and its stories through her eyes, and as a result, I now know that when catastrophe strikes (such as in the case of Goldilocks falling off her bed before the bears arrive), one should simply "pretend that didn't happen."

Introduction

Making Stories "Real"

"Don't you remember? . . ."
   I do remember . . . only Pooh doesn't very well, so that's why he likes having
it told to him again. Because then it's a real story and not just a remembering.

—A. A. Milne (1996, 18)

What is a real story? How might stories come alive and become real for young children? Telling a story requires us to understand and to communicate our perceptions of the story. If we acquire a deep understanding of the plot, characters, setting, problems, solutions, and meanings of new vocabulary words, we can better communicate the story to others. We make the story "real" to our audiences when we add voices, facial expressions, props, and meaning to the retelling. In this book, we'll embark on a journey in teaching young children the art of story retelling.

One child pretends to read a story—a version of story retelling—about Winnie-the-Pooh while another pauses to listen.

The focus of this book is on designing effective and developmentally appropriate teaching strategies for literature-based story retelling with young children. On the one hand, the term *retelling* is defined just as the term implies: telling a story again. Since *telling* is expressed in many ways, this book includes play and the creative arts as modes of communication. Participating in acting out a story with a group is a retelling technique. When a preschooler (who is not able to read) pretends to read a book to another person, the pretend reading serves as story retelling. Stories can be sung, danced, drawn, acted out, played, pretended, and more. For the purpose of this book, the term *story retelling* expands beyond the teacher's flannel board to include the many ways literature-based stories are told and retold by children and their teachers alike.

On the other hand, story retelling *as a teaching strategy* is a loaded term because it necessitates planning, implementing, and assessing to support successful retelling experiences with young children. Further complicating the retelling definition is the awareness that story retelling manifests itself in different ways depending on the age, grade, and developmental level of the child. As a result, the term can often be misinterpreted when implemented in classrooms. This book is designed to demystify the story-retelling experience with young children by tearing the term down into its essential components and benefits, then building it back up again by delineating how story retelling works best in preschool classrooms.

Story retelling as an essential teaching strategy helps teachers understand how young children develop language and literacy skills. Admittedly, teachers of young children in early childhood settings have long created environments that supported story experiences regardless of their teaching philosophies or approaches. Story props and themes related to books are typically woven into multiple centers. A house or grocery store center might include a toy caterpillar to eat through pretend food, a science center may contain a chrysalis and nonfiction books about caterpillars, and the library center might feature *The Very Hungry Caterpillar* by Eric Carle (1997) along with puppets to help children recall, reinvent, and put themselves into the story. Similarly, the flannel board held cutout bears and pigs and other book characters ready for the teacher to use in large-group storytime.

What changed in early childhood settings in recent years is our movement beyond the flannel board into the world of maximizing children's literature to its fullest potential across the curriculum. In the process, we develop a culture of story lovers as we wonder and play and learn. In contrast to the time when preschool and kindergarten teachers were the keepers of stories and flannel boards, we now empower children as story retellers, to support effective literacy learning. Our understandings of the benefits of story retelling have evolved. By respecting children's developmental learning styles and pacing, teachers can effectively present story retelling to children in ways that make a huge impact on their learning—including their vocabulary development.

Focusing on how story retelling is implemented in the early childhood classroom offers many rewards to teachers of young children. Children's backgrounds in language and literacy, story and storytelling, self-regulation and interest, listening skills and engagement, and culture and home experiences all affect how we approach story retelling with young children. Observing and documenting children's expressions of understanding and connections to story through retelling offer data for teachers to analyze growth. This book addresses the complexity of designing developmentally appropriate strategies for young children.

What *are* developmentally appropriate story-retelling strategies for young children? How do we offer play with learning and curriculum? While helping children become successful in story retelling and reenacting, how might teachers protect and nurture the joy and wonder of children and their picture books? This book offers insight into links between how children learn and how to support the development of story-retelling skills.

This book is organized into two parts. Part 1 outlines why we do story retelling with children. It reveals key concepts, benefits, effective teaching strategies, and a framework for developmentally based work with young children. In part 2, you will learn how to implement story retelling with preschoolers as they develop skills in the content areas. The chapters focus on how story retelling affects social-emotional growth, how it supports STEM development, how it can foster deeper understandings of numbers through enactments and retellings, and how assessment can best be used to collect and analyze data.

Beyond the Flannel Board: Story-Retelling Strategies across the Curriculum is written in the spirit of fostering wonder, joy, and exploration of story among children and teachers. My hope is to help teachers successfully implement effective teaching strategies that nurture children's vocabulary, learning dispositions, and experiences with story retelling. Above all, may story retelling nurture a love of story and joyful interactions—fuel for developing passionate, inquisitive readers.

Part 1

Story Retelling: A Developmental Perspective

Bill Martin Jr., author of more than three hundred books for children of all ages, had an idea strike him while riding on a train—so he took out a pen and paper and wrote *Brown Bear, Brown Bear, What Do You See?* in just fifteen minutes. After seeing a poster made by Eric Carle (who was a graphic designer at the time), Martin asked Carle to illustrate the poem as a children's book. Carle completed the illustrations for the book (his first) in one weekend!

I've experienced this beloved story in read-alouds to young children quite frequently in my work in preschool and kindergarten classrooms. It's a popular story, and children listen to it again and again. Recently I came very close to asking a university student (who created elaborate plans) to find another story and delay her read-aloud because I worried that the story was overused. Instead, I chose not to say anything. After all, she put a lot of work into the project and it might be a better learning experience if she found out for herself that this story was used too often with children. You likely know what happened. At yet another read-aloud, I sat there invisibly (as a university supervisor in a preschool) and marveled over the synergy formed when a good teacher, children, and this story are put together. When interviewed by Reading Rockets in 1996 about writing for children, Martin said, "I suppose the satisfaction of writing is that it deals with the chaos of the world and gives it order. And that's all a paragraph does. That's all a story does."

When we prepare for story retelling with young children, we "give it order" by organizing the story so children grasp components; vocabulary so children understand; read-alouds so children engage; and props, visual aids, and storyboards so children are supported.

Story Retelling with Young Children

Stories are retold just about everywhere. Stories are kept in books, and they come alive when read and shared. Stories are also found in stained glass windows at religious services, in works of art at museums, in totem poles, and in the buffalo hides at the National Museum of the American Indian in Washington, DC. A compelling story of Esther Nisenthal Krinitz's pre-Holocaust childhood and subsequent survival was told through her thirty-six embroidered panels, which eventually became a traveling exhibit and book for older students (Krinitz and Steinhardt 2010). It is hypothesized that storytelling was linked to drawings on caves, rocks, and cliffs from times long ago. Stories are expressed through dance, music, movement, art, and drama. Stories are captured in nature when one discovers a beehive in a tree or a decomposed hydrangea on a bush or a chrysalis on a milkweed leaf.

Stories are dramatic! They may be artistic, musical, or full of movement. They make us agonize and celebrate, tremor inside and laugh out loud, worry to pieces and sing for joy. Stories are meant to be *told*; the "telling again" is in the connection between not only the teller and listener but also the dreamer (author and illustrator) and the dream (the story). Stories link us to history and culture. These characteristics of story are central to our read-aloud practices, interactive readings, and other literature-related experiences in classrooms. Literature-based story retelling is a form of storytelling (Morrow 1996).

In the early childhood years, creating a picture often is a legitimate way to share a story or an event. In many aspects of our own lives, we essentially recall, recount, or retell, whether it is through sharing with a friend about a recipe or revealing a few episodes from a favorite book. At base level, story retelling is focused on *what happens when readers or listeners retell a story after hearing or reading it.* Story retelling can be quite demanding of young children, but when it is taught with their development in mind, it becomes fun, joyful, and very educational. Whether retelling is as simple as using facial and/or vocal expressions or

Art and literacy intersect when children create images representing literacy-based and original stories. This teacher made photocopies of the characters on card stock, cut them out and laminated them, glued the characters onto extra-large tongue depressors, and placed them in the class puppet theater with a copy of the book.

as complex as a stage set with costumes, retelling stories with young children is a combination of teacher planning and support, children's emerging and developing skills, and employing the arts in some manner. Story retelling is not simple. It is more than recalling a story or even "a remembering."

In essence, story retelling with young children is a two-part process: (1) what children do when they retell stories, and (2) what teachers do to facilitate competency and support children's developmental growth in both story-retelling skills and concepts. A view of what story retelling *is* and *is not* may further unpack the concept of story retelling in educational settings.

What Is Story Retelling?

Story retelling is, simply, telling a story again in one's own words. It is an overarching term to represent multiple modes of retelling: pretend reading, story acting, story singing, story dancing, miming, and so on. Story retelling is a complex task, especially for young children. To begin with, the reteller must develop a deep understanding of the story. The teller must transcend the level of simply having factual knowledge of a specific story to a level of applying the knowledge in the retelling. Finally, story retelling requires the teller to share the story in an engaging or dramatic way, capturing the spirit or essence of the story in the process. Teachers model story retelling and scaffold children's understanding and expressive language skills. They plan and interact with stories to develop children's understandings of meaning and the important events (or plot) in the story over time. They facilitate understanding of the story and teach literary elements, vocabulary, and comprehension. Teachers are story retellers themselves.

Story retelling is not memorizing, although we know that very young children have a penchant for using verbal memory as a tool for learning. But memorizing a story does not guarantee that children comprehend or understand it. "Retelling does not mean memorizing—it means recounting in the child's own words. . . . Retellings go beyond the literal [recall] and help children focus on a deeper understanding of the text" (Gibson, Gold, and Sgouros 2003, 2). A child must consider what parts of the story are necessary to the overall meaning or wholeness of the story. Children use their language when they retell stories, yet they may "borrow" key vocabulary from the story and include important repeating phrases or words. Children who are proficient at retelling incorporate key sayings, characters, setting, and critical meanings, among other things. In this regard, analysis is part of the story-retelling process. When working with young children, there is value in documenting the

The teacher uses a familiar book, props, and playful interaction to guide the child in a satisfying experience with retelling.

memorizations in retellings and pretend readings. We observe to see if memorization moves toward conceptual understanding, internalizing story maps, cadences, and structures as children develop.

Although story retelling requires the skills inherent in remembering and summarizing, it is not creating a summary of the story. Finding the essentials of the story enables the child to retell the story in a meaningful way through his or her own perspective. Story retelling is a skill, but it also is an art that demands ongoing teaching and preparation.

Story Retelling as Problem Solving

When children retell a story, they discern what is most important and what is least important about the story; problem solving and analysis are involved. They continuously make decisions about the story: determining what comes next, identifying who the characters are, and sharing what happens. Children need time to practice the story with adult facilitation so learning goals are realized. When enacting stories in small groups, social negotiation (who will be which characters, where the tree will be located) offers children problem-solving experiences in the process.

Similarly, teachers problem solve when they select texts for children to retell, differentiate instruction, and identify children's skills and knowledge of story as they retell. Analysis of story-retelling data serves not only in nurturing children's learning strengths and facilitating next steps—it also offers teachers a venue for checking children's story-related vocabulary and comprehension.

The Benefits of Story Retelling

Story retelling with young children is used with both fiction and nonfiction literature. Because story retelling focuses on understanding, vocabulary development, and sequence, it is supportive of children's content learning. When children at a local preschool were learning about social and emotional concepts, their teacher asked them to enact the expressions in the book *Glad Monster, Sad Monster: A Book about Feelings* by Ed Emberley and Anne Miranda (1997). Benefits from using story-retelling strategies with young children across the curriculum abound. Identifying what content knowledge and skills children learn as a result requires documentation and analysis.

We teach the concepts and skills of story retelling because we want children to be able to communicate effectively through retelling, enacting, and recounting. Retelling stories is an application experience—a higher level of learning than answering a question

Children participate in the story and, in doing so, enhance emotions-related vocabulary and dramatic expression.

This child is experiencing gingerbread-scented playdough with rolling pins and cookie cutters to build her conceptual understanding of vocabulary in *The Gingerbread Man.*

pertaining to the story or picking out pictures of the characters. Story retelling also has specific benefits among different ages and developmental ranges. For English-language learners, experiencing a story in many different ways serves to develop comprehension. For example, at a district pre-K, children made gingerbread men out of playdough and baked gingerbread cookies so they could better understand the term "gingerbread" and "cutout cookies." They enacted the story after reading it in small groups, and they created paper gingerbread characters who could say, "Run, run as fast as you can; you can't catch me, I'm the Gingerbread Man." In this regard, story retelling builds bridges between the concrete and symbolic. Related experiences serve as tools for building descriptive vocabulary with adult narration and interaction predominating in early retelling experiences. With young preschoolers, a song or familiar story may be enacted with props, practiced, and retold or sung again and again as part of a story-retelling center. Language development is all about talking, communicating, and interacting in many different ways—and that's what story retelling is.

So, the overarching goal of teaching story retelling to young children is to facilitate the development of effective retellers and communicators; however, in doing this, other benefits follow. Story retelling increases young children's overall development of language and literacy skills (Dunst, Simkus, and Hamby 2012; McGee 2008). Skills development is likely due to the following: "The ability to engage children in a story so deeply that they adopt its literary language, explore the motivation of the characters, and try out multiple ways of being in a character's role, *is* effective in promoting children's literacy and language growth" (McGee, 2008, 157–58).

Effective story retelling requires communication and comprehension. If we understand the meaning or context of what we are listening to or reading, we might use semantic cues to help us figure out a word we might not know—or to predict what might flow next in the reading, helping our fluency. Children who participate in story-retelling learning experiences have opportunities to grow in story-related vocabulary, comprehension, and meaning making, all of which are supportive of reading development and skills (Morrow 2015; Paris and Paris 2007).

The advantages of incorporating story-retelling strategies with toddlers and preschoolers are reported in a meta-analysis conducted by the Center for Early Literacy Learning (Dunst, Simkus, and Hamby 2012). The researchers identified eleven unrelated studies involving a total of 687 toddlers and preschoolers. Although not a "cure-all" for early literacy development, story retelling with young children is emerging as a very useful strategy for building vocabulary and comprehension strategies, according to the authors of the study. Story retelling offers teachers a venue to understand children's perceptions of the story as they practice or play with story in preschool centers or free-play experience, for example.

The language of story differs from the language we use while talking. We are less formal when we talk than while telling a story. Sentences used in talking may be incomplete; unnecessary words might be left out or blended together. In stories, sentences are more predictable. We use the words *the*, *of*, and *and* most frequently when we read—so much so that the words are considered as the most frequently read words in our vocabulary (Fry 2011). Story retelling supports children's understanding of the structure of language found in stories, including experiencing and using frequently read words.

Story-language structure means that an experienced story reteller expects to include the "what" (a person, animal, or thing—the subject) in a sentence. This person, animal, or thing will do something (the action or verb) or be described (adjective) in some way. We develop a sense of written sentence structure before we define subject, verb, adjective, or sentence. Young children "get" story structure with repeated exposure to listening to stories. Syntactic cues help us figure out words and meanings while we read, and are solely based on how language is typically structured in stories. Syntactic cues improve reading fluency (smoothness and pace of reading), which is connected to stronger comprehension while reading. Conducting story retelling with children develops language structures and increases oral language complexity (Morrow 2015).

Story retelling also helps develop a sense of how stories are organized (Morrow 2015; Owocki 1999). In other words, a fictional story generally follows a conceptual map: there is a beginning, middle, and end. We use "Once upon a time" and "They lived happily ever after" in particular places. There are

Children choose to retell *The Very Hungry Caterpillar* together in the Library Center, supporting each other in remembering both the repetitive language and what comes next in the story sequence.

characters, settings, plots, themes, problems, and solutions, and typically we predict that the problem might be resolved closer to the end. Children who have experiences with story retelling internalize the conceptual story map and apply it to the stories they have learned. Morrow found that story retellers in kindergarten and first grade applied structural elements of story when asked to dictate original stories (1996).

This teacher and her young students are organizing for a story enactment by identifying how many children are in the group and how many characters are in the book.

Morrow further reports that story retelling builds summarizing skills. Inevitably, when children retell stories, they must be able to communicate effectively the gist of the story in the retelling (2015). Researchers Brainerd and Renya (1993) studied two types of memory in childhood: verbatim memory (remembering particular, perhaps even exact, details), and gist (the essential idea). The research indicates that children of all ages are capable of obtaining gist. Younger children, however, characteristically tend to "store and retrieve verbatim memory traces," which are defined as "precise details of the information" and are not as enduring as gist (Santrock 2012, 359). Although story retelling is not summarizing, it relies on summarizing skills and capturing gist in the retelling, which may be more challenging for very young children. Knowing that capturing the gist of story is more difficult for young children provides us with further rationale for using a developmental perspective in teaching story-retelling strategies to young children. It also rationalizes using props and visual aids with young children.

Gibson, Gold, and Sgouros suggest that story retelling demonstrates what children remember. They also suggest that story retelling requires children to reconstruct and reflect on text. Children may distinguish words and consider meanings as they reconstruct and retell. "Retellings require children to think more conceptually—to look at the bigger picture—rather than answering specific questions about the text" (2003, 2).

Similarly, Morrow indicates that story retelling promotes organization of thought. Both Morrow and Owocki advocate for quality teacher facilitation in moving children toward organized thinking about story (2015; 1999). Organized thinking about story results from meaningful and intentional discussions over stories. Teachers organize key elements of story when asking about characters or requesting sequence of events, for example.

Story retelling engages children and adults in active discussions (Morrow 1996). A proponent of positive interactions with young children in literacy-rich environments, Morrow promotes modeling responses if children are not able to supply them to teachers. Modeling is an effective strategy to promote language use among nonresponders and English-language learners.

Morrow further indicates that story retelling provides a venue for demonstrating and discussing text-to-self connections (2015). Most preschool children are able to make connections between narrative text and themselves with assistance from their teachers. Making connections builds interest and investment in the learning process. Facilitating active story-related discussions that connect to children's lives are at the heart of teaching for meaning.

The benefits I've described above serve as rationale for implementing story retelling with young children. Similarly, an awareness of story-retelling limitations assists teachers as they plan for effective learning.

Limitations to Implementing Story Retelling with Young Children

Story retelling is beneficial to children, but there are particular issues in implementing effective strategies that pertain to young children and how they learn. One primary limitation of implementing story retelling with young children is in the lack of information about story-retelling pedagogy: the understanding of where children are developmentally and how to teach them effectively. A misconception of what encompasses story retelling complicates how we know where children are developmentally. The focus in recent years has moved away from the pedagogy of story retelling to the assessment of story retelling. Due to the lack of resources for preschool teachers, story retelling may involve quickly asking a child to retell a story after listening for the first time. In this approach, there is no way for the child to develop skills or deep meaning. Developing story-retelling skills in young children is complex and multilayered. Teachers need to determine where children are developmentally—from simple to complex retellings and from emerging to proficient competencies.

A second limitation is related to the heterogeneous populations served in classrooms. Children in preschool settings are often grouped in multiage classrooms, holding diverse backgrounds in literacy and vocabulary acquisition. To differentiate instruction effectively, teachers of young children rely on an understanding of how children learn effectively according to developmental continuums (see chapter 4). Benefits of and research on effective story-retelling development in young children guide teachers' planning and facilitation for effective learning among the populations they serve.

A third issue in implementing story retelling with young children is that their language development differs greatly. It is well documented that children's early vocabulary development is typically related to parental and caregiver interaction. Hart and Risley compared children's exposure to words in families among varied socioeconomic status levels between the ages of seven months and three years of age, where they found an established pattern of language development that could predict the trajectory of their future use of language (2003). The study's subjects were children from three distinct levels of socioeconomic status (SES): high, middle/lower, and poverty. Among their findings was a profound comparison of average word use by families across the traditional SES levels. An extrapolated data set was described as a "30 million word gap by age three" (2003, 4). In other words, children who are in poverty hear less than one-third of the words children experience in high SES families.

They describe this phenomenon as an "early catastrophe" regarding language development across the socioeconomic strata (4).

Young children's grasp of language, whether it is first or second language acquisition, impacts how they will navigate literacy learning and story retelling. Children acquire receptive vocabulary prior to expressive vocabulary. Story retelling demands expression. The nature of varied language levels among children in early childhood classrooms impacts how teachers implement strategies to scaffold children toward larger vocabularies. Story retelling from a developmental perspective serves as a scaffold and motivator to facilitate language and meaning in young children. Hart and Risley's study also compels us to use positive interactions, modeling, and encouragement as we interact with children in story-retelling activities.

Next, children's varying exposure to literature prior to entering school challenges teachers to differentiate story retelling with young children. I recall taking a group of undergraduate teacher candidates to a local, district-run early childhood developmental center for family literacy field experiences with children and families. Families whose children used this center were from varied backgrounds: refugees, immigrants, English-language learners, Caucasian children, and an urban Native American preschool. At the end of each field visit, families were given a copy of the children's book that served as a common experience for all the centers in the "family book celebrations." One mother shared with a teacher candidate her appreciation for the children's book. This was the first book she had ever owned. Children who have little to no exposure to language or children's literature, those who are learning English as a second language, and children who do not share mainstream culture may be perceived as deficit oriented because they may need more modeling, coaching, scaffolding, and support in developing story-retelling skills. Increasingly, however, teachers counter such deficit models of the child by learning about children's cultural backgrounds, knowledge, and skills, or their "funds of knowledge" (Moll et al. 1992/2001, 132). The researchers indicate the following:

> Our analysis of funds of knowledge represents a positive (and we argue, realistic) view of households as containing ample cognitive and cultural resources with great, *potential* utility in classroom instruction (italics by the researchers). . . . This view of households, we should mention, contrasts sharply with prevailing and accepted perceptions of working-class families as somehow disorganized socially and deficient intellectually; perceptions that are well accepted and rarely challenged in the field of education and elsewhere. (Moll et al. 1992/2001, 134)

Alternatively, the familiar story of *The Three Little Pigs*—a common one for story retelling because of its popularity—might offer a child multiple versions with the same story, thus complicating the retelling for the young learner. *The Three Little Pigs* could also pose issues for the English-language learner or a child who has never heard the story. A recent trip to a local independent bookseller in our city produced twenty-seven versions of the story (a quick search of a popular online bookseller yielded far more than that number). Although the story holds similarities across the versions, differences exist. This leads to an issue of how much background a child has in story and exposure to stories—and what impact these exposures have on how children choose to retell a story. It also leads to questions about the role cultural background has on story-retelling implementations in the classroom.

Diversity in cultural upbringing in American classrooms does impact children's language and literacy development. Our Midwestern city's school district enrolls children representing over one hundred languages as their first language—none of which are English. Differences in cultural values in language and literacy have an impact on developing story narratives among young children (Anderson et al. 2013). A funds-of-knowledge approach recognizes what children bring to schools as strengths: their culture, background knowledge, and skills (Gonzalez, Moll, and Amanti 2005). A funds-of-knowledge perspective compels teachers to first learn about families in their own contexts and then design classroom environments and curricula with elements of children's cultural backgrounds, knowledge, and skills woven within. Home visits and seeking out children's or families' favorite stories (handed down, cultural, oral, traditional, or literature-based) are natural ways to weave in funds of knowledge in the context of story retelling.

Next, young children may not be interested in a particular story or story retelling and don't engage in story retelling at the time we may ask them to do so. Or they may retell a story in order of importance to them as opposed to retelling a story in sequential order. Rather than considering this as a miscue or error, teachers who understand the role development plays in learning celebrate this finding and document the retelling as a marker in the child's story-retelling progression—good assessment data demonstrating the role that self plays in expression of story. Taking creative license with retellings during playtime or at centers could be viewed by those not aware of the developmental need for play as a limitation to story retelling with young children. Those who understand why children need play will see this as an opportunity for children to make meaning (Welsch 2008). When children are not interested in the story, they may actually have fully developed story-retelling skills and knowledge, but it hasn't emerged in this particular retelling—another reason why assessment over time is crucial. The issue of child interest plays into problems with assessment in general (more on assessment is found in chapter 8).

Young children use play as a means for learning and coping at times, which offers interesting opportunities for teachers. Stories retold through a child's perspective during play episodes may take a story in a direction not found in the book. Creepy Carrots may visit Aunt Megan's wedding for a reason during an open-ended playtime (Reynolds 2012). Although not in the story, this re-imagining may serve an important role in working out three-year-old Charlotte's concerns over an impending change when her aunt will soon marry and relocate to another town. It is Charlotte's way of making important connections to the text while serving as a coping strategy at the same time.

Finally, older children who love to memorize may find story retelling in

This child pretends while dressing up as a community helper—his enactments during play enable him to explore roles he is learning about in large- and small-group work.

their own words very challenging. As mentioned earlier, story retelling is not memorizing, yet in early childhood, we acknowledge memorization of story as part of the developmental process in some children and related to verbatim memory representations mentioned earlier in the chapter. To alleviate memorization in story retelling with young children, model and encourage children to tell stories in their own words. Ask comprehension and elaboration questions to share value in meaning as opposed to "getting the words right," which essentially conflicts with messages we send about reading (where we do wish children to strive for word accuracy).

Issues and limitations in implementing story retelling with young children may be capitalized on in various ways. If you are using large multiage groupings, be aware of the research demonstrating that working with small groups of three to four children in story retelling/enacting is most effective (McGee 2008). Language-rich classroom environments with quality teacher and peer interactions/responses enhance language development. Although children's backgrounds include varied exposures to literature, teachers capitalize on the interactive read-aloud experience to create a common experience in the classroom. Lack of child interest may be countered by offering times during the day for children to freely explore their play, social, and cognitive interests and also by presenting children with high-quality books that appear to be written for the sole purpose of engaging and entertaining children. Respecting the rhythm of the child counters lack of interest as well. By observing children during play, teachers capitalize on documenting how stories connect to children's thinking and processing skills while also capitalizing on teachable moments in the process.

Retelling Stories with Language and Understanding

Teachers who work with young children plan experiences designed to develop language and understanding. As in the example below, children are encouraged when teachers, parents, and caregivers repeat their words and offer new concepts and words with encouragement or joyful voices. Integral to the work of early childhood educators is the development of language, which teachers use many differentiation strategies to achieve. Children between the ages of three and five represent a wide developmental span. In addition to the span in ages and developmental levels, preschool children represent varied cultures, socioeconomic statuses, and experiences. Teachers must plan learning experiences that provide growth for all children. The need for continuous

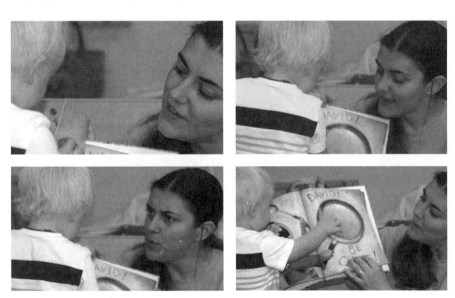

The teacher stops reading and says with surprise, "The pan *does* look like a ball!" The toddler repeats, "Ball!" and pats the page again. His teacher says, "Yes, ball!" They make eye contact and smile as though sharing an inside joke. The child says, "Ball," followed by, "no, no, no." The teacher repeats, "Ball, no, no, no, David!" Later, the teacher shares her joy over the incident, the first time the child labeled a picture in a book with her. (McWilliams, June 2015 research notes)

Recognizing that stories exist in classroom routines, a teacher posted photographs with labels in top-to-bottom sequence for children as both a support for remembering and a mechanism for reflection on the routine.

differentiation and individualization among young children is one of many reasons why teaching in small groups is more effective than large-group instruction.

Because the development of children's language and understanding is always on our agenda whether we're teaching about math concepts or about watering the class plants, teachers of young children continuously seek interaction with their students. Teachers ask questions about paintings and inquire about the rocks children take to school. They tap into Maya's excitement over her new puppy and try to find out more about why Antonio had a hard time separating from his mother today. Teachers seek out stories from children and learn about their lives and their interests. Children's stories are not limited to conversations with teachers; their stories emerge in play, in art, in the block center—everywhere.

Teachers create environments to nurture stories that are relevant to children and their lives. Engaging young children in participative stories, recording their own stories and acting them out, and documenting stories in children's art when they emerge are some of the many ways teachers support language development and meaning in early childhood classrooms. By starting off with an understanding of children's language and learning needs, we are better able to select what to teach (the content) and how to teach it (the pedagogy).

Understanding Children's Language Learning Needs in the Preschool Years

Early childhood teachers ascertain "starting points" by determining children's current knowledge and interests through observation, asking families, and other assessment strategies. Children develop an internal understanding of language before they are able to communicate words and concepts to others. Some preschoolers may know concepts or vocabulary but, for various reasons, do not speak very often. Understanding what one hears is known as a *receptive vocabulary*. When children label a concept or share their comprehension in words with others, they have developed an *expressive vocabulary*. This is one reason why teachers constantly model vocabulary.

Beginning with what children accomplish independently helps us in responsive teaching. We scaffold children to higher levels of skill and understanding in developmentally appropriate ways: with small steps or hops instead of large leaps. Similarly, we build depth of understanding by widening concepts with experiences. By encompassing a concept with hands-on experiences and interaction over time, children develop deep understandings and make important connections.

Carefully selected literature for the young child offers opportunities for language development. Typically, picture books offer more sophisticated vocabulary words than talking—one reason why our work with reading to young children often involves teaching story-related language and vocabulary. The wording in picture books may be beyond a child's typical interactions but useful to learn because they are words that will be encountered frequently when the child learns to read. Authors of children's books use words typically not spoken to children, words that are, in fact, beyond basic words. Beck, McKeown, and Kucan categorized words typically held by literate people into a tier system that helps us make sense of vocabulary instruction (2013). Tier One words are basic and frequently spoken (such as *happy* or *car*). High-quality, simple concept books written expressly for infants and toddlers often rely on basic words. Tier Two words are also frequently used but richer than Tier One words (*joyful* or *automobile*). The authors call Tier Two words "sophisticated" and for children to use sophisticated words, they need "robust" vocabulary instruction (Beck, McKeown, and Kucan 2013, 3). Finally, Tier Three words are infrequently used and often apply to specific disciplines.

We help children develop sophisticated words by providing child-friendly definitions and helping children make connections to their own lives. When teachers select quality books that appeal to young learners' interests and interact over the content, they expand vocabulary. Selecting the right book with sophisticated words is an important part of planning for story retelling. Teachers look at issues of length, complexity, illustration quality, child interest, and vocabulary (see chapter 4 for more on book selection). A thorough understanding of stories helps children in the story-retelling process.

Three language-development teaching goals go into our read-aloud work with children: (1) using intentional oral language in our story conversations, (2) developing listening comprehension, and (3) identifying potential vocabulary words and their meanings in stories. The first two will be discussed as teaching strategies for story retelling in chapter 3. Generally accepted constructs for developing vocabulary follow here.

Teaching Story-Related Vocabulary to Support Retelling

When teachers identify and teach vocabulary words found in stories, they support young children in successful story-retelling experiences (McGee 2008). Researchers indicate that words are learned over the passage of time through meaningful and repeated exposures to vocabulary (Neuman 2011; Harris, Golinkoff, and Hirsh-Pasek 2011). Children need many experiences with words and their meanings in authentic ways to really grow their vocabularies. In preschool, just as with teaching English-language learners, developing vocabulary goes beyond talk and into the world of experiential learning, relying on teaching strategies that put hands-on materials and other resources in the learning environment. Using authentic materials, examining phenomena of study, and watching a video are several strategies teachers use to build vocabulary. Intentionality in planning plays into the effective teaching and learning of vocabulary words.

Both early literacy and child development researchers advocate intentional and strong emphasis on vocabulary instruction for read-aloud experiences (Harris, Golinkoff, and Hirsh-Pasek 2011; McGee and Schickedanz 2007; Neuman 2011). Key characteristics emerge from the research and literature on teaching vocabulary to young children:

- Identify potential vocabulary words ahead of the read-aloud.
- Teach the definition of vocabulary words through explicit (direct) instruction and provide application experiences through implicit (contextual) teaching.
- Repeatedly look for opportunities to use the word with children even after the story is no longer a focus.
- Provide experiences for children to use the words authentically to promote depth of processing.
- Select stories and words that interest children.
- Teach vocabulary in child-friendly terms with interactive and responsive strategies rather than using passive strategies.
- Recognize that vocabulary learning helps children learn about grammar and vice versa.
- Monitor children's progress by documenting their growth in curriculum-related vocabulary.

Let's look at how these characteristics drive preschool teaching strategies for vocabulary development in read-aloud experiences, which in turn support children's story-retelling experiences.

Identify Potential Vocabulary Words

Researchers advocate for establishing vocabulary focus words prior to reading to even our youngest learners (McGee and Schickedanz 2007; Neuman 2011). Draw attention to vocabulary words before reading (using pictures in the book as applicable or by discussing or enacting). The process doesn't end with identification, however. Effective instruction includes isolating the words and drawing attention to them while reading. Typically, teachers new to teaching vocabulary to preschoolers begin with one focus word per story and slowly build toward higher numbers of vocabulary with future read-alouds, one at a time. They base the number of vocabulary words per story on preschoolers' stamina and developmental levels. Beauchat, Blamey, and Philippakos suggest focusing on one or two words per story for preschool children and two to three for kindergarten and first grade (2012). McGee and Schikedanz, when writing about read-alouds with three- to six-year-old children, note that they select between five and ten words or phrases to analyze and explain while reading (2007).

To complete the vocabulary identification process, teachers associate words with meanings. Whether the definition comes from a children's dictionary or is one the teacher creates with her students in mind, the definitions should be clear, using child-oriented terminology—often including Tier One wording so children can relate. Effective vocabulary teaching includes communicating meaning through explicit teaching.

Use Explicit and Implicit Teaching

In explicit teaching—also called direct teaching—teachers tell children what words they are focusing on, and they give clear and precise child-oriented meanings. Include a picture card or prop or the real thing (concrete materials) to represent the vocabulary word if feasible; act out the vocabulary word if it is a verb. Teachers offer children opportunities to discuss vocabulary words and definitions to develop deeper meanings through sharing perspectives. Text-to-self connections, where children associate the vocabulary word with something in their lives, are particularly relevant for preschool students. Children need opportunities to contribute examples of the word usage from their own lives and apply those words contextually.

Implicit teaching is an indirect or contextual way of learning. In implicit teaching, teachers draw out vocabulary words from the context of reading. Teachers might model how they would figure out what the word means within the reading scenario, thereby modeling contextual cues. Additionally, teachers offer children environmental contexts and suggestions for applying their new vocabulary words in the classroom through free play, story-retelling centers, props, the creative arts, books in the block center, and so on. Using new

While children are "shelling corn" during the fall (a popular fall sensory table experience in Nebraska), the teacher seizes the opportunity to expand on vocabulary and concept development related to autumn-themed books and experiences: *shelling, husking, shucking, corn, cob, dried corn, feed for animals,* and *seed.*

vocabulary words in the context of story retelling is an important application experience for young children that helps them remember new words. Both explicit and implicit teaching are needed for effective vocabulary development in the early childhood years (Bridges et al. 2012; Harris, Golinkoff, and Hirsh-Pasek 2011; Neuman 2011). Children need clear information about word meanings, and they learn words best in meaningful contexts.

Children Learn through Repetition

Learning happens in layers. We offer repetition while teaching young children so they can revisit concepts and gather depth of knowledge based on their new schemas. When we repeat a story, we're not really repeating the same things over and over again, but instead, we're revisiting through different angles or alternative perspectives, or in greater depth than before.

Enacting the story *A Box Can Be Many Things* (Rau 1997), children and teachers use the book to help them follow the sequence of how a box may be turned into several different make-believe things and enact the meanings of words such as *flip, punch holes,* and *rip.*

Vocabulary development similarly mimics this process of layering on knowledge and spiraling through meanings. Repeated exposure to vocabulary instruction is a characteristic of teaching for meaning. Go back to the context of the word in the story to talk about it again after reading, share how the word is used in other contexts, or talk about the word in relation to children's own lives (text-to-self connections). Neuman, researching vocabulary development in kindergarten and primary grades, found that although teachers addressed vocabulary in school while reading, they seldom *repeated* meaningful vocabulary experiences (2011). This is problematic because children need repeated exposures to effectively learn and apply new vocabulary words. Just as Hart and Risley cite the importance of parental impact on children's vocabulary learning (2003), relationships between teacher input and child vocabulary output exist also in early school environments (Harris, Golinkoff, and Hirsh-Pasek 2011). Children need frequent and quality-oriented exposure to vocabulary instruction—a principle that is at the core of the shared/interactive reading discussion that is found in the third chapter.

Promote Depth of Processing

To understand the concept of *depth of processing*, we must look at two types of knowledge: factual and conceptual. *Factual knowledge* is simply content; it could involve rote memorization. A child might tell a teacher that an insect has six legs, three body parts, antennae, and sometimes wings, for example. The child has factual knowledge of the word *insect*. Neuman indicates that this type of knowledge isn't enough. She offers differences between factual knowledge (or rote memorization of words) that might be placed in short-term memory, and a depth-of-processing knowledge, which is how conceptual understanding is developed (2011). Centers-based learning, such as dramatic play, the creative arts, library, and science, is helpful here, as is inquiry-oriented teaching and learning—when children interact with each other to ask questions, find out answers, make observations, create hypotheses, experiment, solve problems, use literature and media as sources of information, and report to others. Neuman suggests that learning activities for young children who use "play, drama, and problem solving tasks" will create longer-lasting and more relevant meanings (360), all of which require children to use their knowledge of vocabulary.

Similarly, Harris, Golinkoff, and Hirsh-Pasek propose that guided play offers a venue for effective vocabulary acquisition as opposed to memorization (2011). Guided play is a strategy that enables teacher facilitation of learning objectives in the context of play, engagement, interaction, and discovery. Depth of processing brings about *conceptual knowledge*: an ability to express or demonstrate why, explain, and articulate cause-and-effect relationships. In this case, a child might demonstrate knowledge of an insect by applying the definition to an illustration or a three-dimensional sculpture out of clay. He may retell a nonfiction passage about insects using a model or real insect as props in the retelling. Our overarching goal in teaching vocabulary is developing conceptual understanding through depth of processing. The bottom line is that depth-of-processing vocabulary is acquired when children have opportunities to experiment, play, and practice with words, and they get these opportunities not from discussing or memorizing vocabulary but from conducting inquiry projects, enacting or retelling stories with props, creating with art and recyclable or repurposed materials, exploring, playing, and experiencing.

Teachers and parents may think that children have acquired conceptual understanding or depth in processing when a child states a definition of a word or successfully picks that definition out in a multiple-choice test in elementary school. It's possible these children have deep understandings—but also possible they may not. Factual knowledge typically precedes conceptual understanding. In my work with children, I've learned that a child (grades K–2) can state the definition of an insect or tell the five senses but may not be able to demonstrate conceptual understanding by applying—either through illustration or demonstration—an accurate portrayal or discussion of insects or the senses.

Offer Curriculum That Appeals to Children's Interests

Just as children learn through play, they also learn vocabulary more effectively if adults offer words based on children's interests. Similarly, stories that interest children will have longevity for repeated readings and analysis. Relating a story to the child's interest or personal experience (a text-to-self connection) is an effective practice during the read-aloud experience (Dunst, Simkus, and Hamby 2012; Harris, Golinkoff, and Hirsch-Pasek 2011; Morrow 1996, 2015).

Teach with Interactive and Responsive Strategies

Interaction and responsiveness in teaching are additional characteristics of quality vocabulary teaching and learning. "Adults who take turns, share periods of joint focus and express positive affect when interacting with young children provide children with the scaffolding needed to facilitate language and cognitive growth" (Harris, Golinkoff, and Hirsh-Pasek 2011, 54). Teachers ask why (analyze), how, and what-do-you-mean (explain) questions. Listen to children's answers and offer responses that either validate children's understanding or take them to the next level. Responses that include acknowledgment of what the child accomplished ("You used a very unhappy voice and facial expression when your Beatrice puppet said 'Mine' and grabbed all the balloons from the clown") will mean more than praise. Sensitive interactions and responses are beneficial to language development.

Vocabulary and Grammar Are Connected

Because children's literature is typically written in complete sentences, it offers children models of grammar and sophisticated, wonderful, rich words. The act of retelling a story encourages teachers and children to get into their story voices and use the language of story while making it their own. The research tells us that vocabulary learning and grammatical development are reciprocal processes (Harris, Golinkoff, and Hirsh-Pasek 2011). This is important for story listeners and readers because language structures help us clarify meaning in a vague or unknown word. It is also important to retelling stories because the reteller must use meanings and language structures to communicate the story to others. This offers implications on the importance of the story read-aloud while children are in the midst of developing vocabulary and grammar. Scaffold children's vocabulary and grammar (through analysis, clarifications, direct teaching, and repeating their words plus one new concept or word or meaning) while interacting, reading, and retelling. Teachers model being great readers: we model our thinking strategies while reading (called think-out-loud strategies) and engaging story retellers.

Assess Progress

Finally, monitoring the progress of children's vocabulary development is essential to growth (Neuman 2011). Although assessments such as the Peabody Picture Vocabulary Test, which measures receptive vocabulary (Dunn and Dunn 2007), are helpful to teachers, Neuman recommends vocabulary assessments focused on classroom curriculum because they are more accurate in determining vocabulary development specific to the classroom. Essentially, documenting children's usage and explanations of curricular-related vocabulary offers us ways to find out if children are growing in vocabulary.

Story retelling demands that children understand and apply vocabulary effectively. When teachers ask children for elaborations of story-related vocabulary, observe children applying vocabulary in play, and observe vocabulary usage while story retelling, teachers gain insight into where children are in developing understandings of concepts and words. Teachers find opportunities to model and encourage vocabulary usage across the classroom environment.

When teachers or parents engage children in dialogue about the text through questioning, making connections, and elaborating on vocabulary, children's expressive vocabulary increases overall. Similarly, story retelling supports vocabulary development by offering application contexts that are especially effective when teachers are coaching and/or using guided play strategies.

Successful story retelling with young children relies on their understanding of vocabulary found in the literature. But it also encompasses understanding the organizational structures of stories and information. Next, we'll explore how to help organize story retelling for young children by analyzing the structures of text.

Before reading about pumpkins, this teacher revisited the dissected pumpkin and the vocabulary of pumpkins generated earlier in the week with children. Exploring concrete items is an effective strategy for developing vocabulary.

Using Structures of Text to Organize and Support Story Retelling

Children's literature is our primary source of stories in literature-based story retelling. Fictional (narrative) organizational structures differ from the ways nonfiction (expository text) is organized. Fictional organizational structures, also called story maps, are generally similar to each other (and likewise nonfiction books are organized in similar ways). This knowledge of story structure and organization helps us with making meaning when we listen and we read. But this knowledge of story structure—that it exists and that the structures of fiction and nonfiction are different—comes with experiencing different types of text. It comes with a thoughtful guide who helps us navigate the world of books.

Young children are just getting started in exploring story and nonfiction texts, and they aren't in a position to effectively analyze stories for their organizational structures before retelling. When teachers provide the story's organization, they support children in becoming successful with story retelling. Ways to provide story organization to children are varied. Here are a few examples: offer children prompts (such as questions) while retelling; include access to the book while learning how to retell the story; provide specific props or visual aids that serve as reminders of key parts of the story; and create a simple story map on poster paper (or, as in the case of one teacher, make a story path on which children place their props as they walk along and retell the story). Organizing the story supports children in the retelling.

Before we look into how fiction and nonfiction stories are typically organized, it should be said that not all literature for the young child is organized in the typical way. In early childhood, literature is inclusive of songs, which may or may not have much of a story line. Concept books abound and include topics such as counting, emotions, ABCs, or balls. They have no problems, solutions, goals, or meeting of goals. Sometimes authors will reveal concepts through an organized structure, however, such as using a calendar to share the concept of eggs hatching or metamorphosis. Other times, simple stories are told as add-on or cumulative structures—*I Know an Old Lady Who Swallowed a Fly*—or in circles—*If You Give a Mouse a Cookie* (Numeroff 1985).

Identifying Narrative Text Structures

Retelling a specific fictional story requires the child to apply the story's important vocabulary and its meaning to her overall understanding of how stories are told: the structure or conceptual map of narrative text. Many template versions of fictional story maps exist, from simple (beginning, middle, and end) to complex (all story elements, problems, solutions, and themes). The Recommended Resources section at the end of this book demonstrate how story structures are used to create an organizing visual aid for retelling with young children. Our mainstream conceptual map of a typical fictional story includes a setting, characters, plot, theme, beginning, middle, end, and problem and solution:

- The underlying simple structure of narrative text is in sequence: beginning, middle, and end that flow linearly.

- The beginning of a story is often associated with special wording such as "Once upon a time," "Long ago and far away," or "There once was a...." Often we are introduced to all the main characters and provided knowledge of the setting, and we may get hints of a problem. Otherwise, the problem (or goal) emerges near the middle.

- The middle of the story typically is where the problem (or endeavor to reach a goal) heightens. The middle often culminates at the climax of the story (if there is one) where problems are resolved (or the goal is met).

- The end of the story lets us know what happens after the climax— and "they all lived happily ever after, the end"—with special wording for the end of the story, especially in fairy tales.

- A story has a sense of place and time: the setting.

- A story has characters who are engaged in the action.

- A story has a plot: the essential causal events.

- A story includes a theme: the overall big idea the author is trying to communicate to the reader, a moral, or a lesson learned.

- A story could have repeating phrases or recurring events that must be retold over and over again to keep the integrity of the story intact.

- Stories carry a specific language structure that differs from the way we typically hold conversations.

Not all stories follow the aforementioned European narrative map. With an influx of immigrants, refugees, and other second-language learners in our schools, knowledge of cultural variance especially found in traditional stories is crucial. It requires teachers to let go of their long-held assumptions that all fiction follows a similar pattern. For example, Resnick and Snow indicate that in some cultures, the story is mapped more as circles around the theme in various ways (common in Latino and African American stories) as opposed to a more sequential European map (2009). The authors note on the other hand that some Japanese stories are more succinct than European versions, suggesting that the stories are "concise accounts that mirror the artistic precision of haiku poems" (10).

Identifying Structures in Expository Text

The word *expository* is derived from the word *expose,* which means "to reveal." Expository text is nonfiction writing, and in the case of biography, memoir, or history, expository text could appear in a similar manner as narrative text. Expository text explains, informs, describes, defines, and instructs. Children typically come into initial contact with expository text when they check out books from the library about animals or dinosaurs, places to visit, or historic/ contemporary figures. In the early childhood years, expository text shows up in science or social studies (and other content-related) textbooks or literature. Young children need experiences with expository texts in interactive read-alouds (connected to inquiry-oriented projects or interest-driven searches) for the sake of navigating reading for information when they are older.

Children engaged with nonfiction benefit from understanding the organizational structure of expository text. They benefit from knowing that expository text is organized into big ideas as headings with details to follow. Captions are under pictures. What they are reading is true information as best as can be told. Likewise, teachers help young students organize their nonfiction retellings (sharing information) under similar structures. The many content-area disciplines organize information differently; examples of typical organizational structures are as follows:

- Describing by stating the overall topic, offering big ideas, and following with details for each big idea. Often this is a mainstay with our youngest learners because this version of expository text is so compatible with observation and working with real materials (such as flowers and insects).

- Offering cause and effect

- Persuading by making a statement, giving the pros and cons of an issue, and taking a position

- Comparing and contrasting

- Presenting problems and solutions

- Asking questions and answering them

- Providing sequential information (as in historic events or describing a procedure)

Teaching goals for developing story retellers align with objectives for cultivating conceptual understandings of language, story vocabulary, and meanings. Nurturing story retellers includes teaching concepts of narrative and expository texts (organization and core concepts). Facilitating proficiencies in story retelling offers teachers a venue for teaching vocabulary and developing conceptual understanding through experiential learning. In this regard, we create coherence between and among what we teach and what we expect children to learn. We focus our teaching on specific outcomes while scaffolding children's learning.

Planning Read-Alouds for Effective Story Retelling

Mrs. Whitmore teaches children in her inclusive class who range from three to five years old and are part of district-combined pre-K/early childhood special education, Head Start, and Title One programs. She uses story retelling regularly in her classroom. She's mostly interested in building language and vocabulary because many of her students exhibit needs in that area. After reading *The Itsy Bitsy Spider* by Rebecca and Ed Emberley aloud, singing the song, discussing vocabulary, and modeling retelling with props, Mrs. Whitmore sets up a story-retelling center so children can practice with props. "Use your words. I want to hear you using your words," says the pre-K teacher, videotaping them to upload in an electronic portfolio for later analysis.

Linking a song to a children's book as in *The Itsy Bitsy Spider* offers children an experience beyond the song because vocabulary is explained through pictures. The father-daughter Emberley team depicts the song in all its simplicity

Children use a story-in-a-box created by their teacher. *The Itsy Bitsy Spider* is a popular story to retell because it helps draw out meaning of words such as *waterspout* and positional words in space. Use of props during small-group time gives teachers opportunities to check understanding while guiding story retelling.

yet provides a more complex spider than young children are typically used to seeing—one with multiple eyes (2013). Mrs. Whitmore created props made of paper (cloud and sun), a paper tube (the water spout), yarn (the rain), and a pom-pom spider. The song-storybook has a cognitive focus on vocabulary of the story and on positions in space (up and down). By enacting the story and through encouragement to "use [their] words," children *become* the story and in the process gather deeper understanding.

Interactive read-alouds create a common experience in the classroom and offer large-group, small-group, and individual teaching opportunities. Having an ongoing story-retelling center enables children to revisit old stories and practice new ones as a choice activity. The center gives Mrs. Whitmore a place to work with small, flexible groups of children in story retelling. It also offers a natural venue to seamlessly assess children's progress after they have had opportunities to practice in centers and play freely with props.

Our primary objectives for developing story retellers change as children gain experience in language and literacy proficiencies. An understanding of big-picture read-aloud strategies may assist teachers of even our youngest learners to effectively implement the foundation of story retelling: language development and meaning. Read-alouds with young children are planned to include before-, during-, and after-reading experiences.

Before Reading: Introducing the Story to Children

Selecting the story is the first step for the teacher when planning for story retelling. Choosing stories relevant for young children is partly dependent on where children are developmentally and what interests them. (Story selection is addressed more fully in chapter 4.) After selecting the story or nonfiction literature, gather or create props and/or visual aids and include a storage plan so the book and props are always together. Once selected, the story is introduced and read to children for absolute, pure *enjoyment* (Isabel Baker, personal conversation, 2013; McGee and Schickedanz 2007). McGee and Schickedanz indicate that vocabulary support, questions, and analytical comments are used by teachers in this initial reading to support children's first understanding of the story.

Before-reading teaching strategies used for story retelling with young children include best practices in teaching reading to young learners. When introducing the book, teachers are encouraged to (a) keep it short, (b) keep it focused, and (c) keep it interactive. The introduction is intentionally planned as a conversation about the book to help draw children's interests into the story and prepare them for successful comprehension.

The more the introduction supports story-retelling skills, the more effective it will be. Identifying the problem, comprehending the story, understanding story structure, articulating sequence, identifying characters, using expression while communicating the story, and discerning other elements of story are among the objectives of the introduction. Focusing on the role of the author or illustrator (and their bodies of work) with young children—though an important content area (and connection) that should be developed in young learners during read-alouds—is less productive in an early story-retelling introduction than focusing on vocabulary, story problem, sequence, or characters.

When the story is introduced for story-retelling purposes, teachers often focus on content vocabulary by asking children for their observations of illustrations related to specific vocabulary—pointing out potential unknown words in a picture walk through the book. Teachers may choose, on the other hand, to read the title and wonder out loud about the story inside, asking for responses—again, preparing children for understanding the story while modeling a think-out-loud strategy. Similarly, teachers might ask children for their predictions about the book based on the cover. Another option is to engage children in talking about peritextual features—those images and text surrounding the story or nonfiction text, such as the title page, copyright page, and endpapers—to advance the teaching objective.

Teachers of young children intentionally plan for identifying unfamiliar vocabulary and introducing it before reading. McGee and Schickedanz indicate that before they read a book out loud, they identify five to ten words or phrases drawn from the story that will be highlighted or defined while reading. They call this "inserting vocabulary support" (2007, 744). Alternatively, as noted in chapter 2, Beauchat, Blamey, and Phillippakos suggest one to two new vocabulary words per reading in pre-K; for kindergarten and first grade, two to three vocabulary words per reading are appropriate (2012). I suggest teachers gauge the number of vocabulary focus words to what they believe children can handle and need.

Morrow suggests letting children know they will be retelling the story while introducing it. She believes in making learning goals transparent during the introduction (2015). For example, if a teacher wants children to interact in a discussion about the problem in the story after they listen (or read), she should use her introduction to encourage children to be ready to discuss the problem afterward. In table 3.1, characteristics of introducing stories before reading (for the purpose of preparing for story retelling) are summarized.

Table 3.1: What Teachers Do: Before-Reading Strategies

Strategy	Explanation/Sample Strategies
Planning: Select the story	• Select a book that offers great potential for story retelling. • Select a book that meets children's interests and sets them up for success. • Offer books that meet children's developmental needs (repetitive and familiar stories offer a good start for novice retellers)
Planning: Select a focused learning objective	• Decide the focus of the read-aloud and plan coherent questions to meet the learning objective throughout (in before-, during-, and after-reading experiences) • Examples of read-aloud focus areas are vocabulary, problem identification, and sequencing.
Planning: Gather materials	• Create or collect props/visual aids and story maps or organizational structures before reading to assist in retelling.

(continued from previous page)

Strategy	Explanation/Sample Strategies
Planning: Identify vocabulary before reading	• Anticipate vocabulary enhancements prior to reading as well as vocabulary needed during the analysis of the text (McGee and Schickedanz 2007). • Create a child-oriented definition (Beauchat, Blamey, and Philippakos 2012).
Planning: Create short introductions	• Lengthy before-reading conversations are not productive with very young children in large groups.
Introductions: Facilitate problem identification	• Pre-K children are less likely to center their thinking on the problem of the story (McGee and Schickedanz 2007). • Introduce the potential for a problem by setting the stage for children to observe and analyze the problem in the story; help them discover the problem.
Introductions: Develop vocabulary	• Discuss illustrations that depict vocabulary words. • Conduct picture walks that allow for vocabulary conversations. • Relate a personal experience with a vocabulary word. • Show the page depicting the vocabulary word and discuss before reading. • Increase levels of understanding each time the word is discussed.
Introductions: Focus on the learning objective	• Choose features that support the objective and interest children. • Share the teaching and learning focus (objective) with children. • Discuss the title and offer context or background as needed. • Redirect children to story-related responses as needed in the case of off-task commentary (Morrow 1996). • Draw attention to details on the cover as they relate to the objective. • Use a picture-walk strategy to help children focus on the objective before reading. • Ask for predictions.
Introductions: Inform children of retelling	• Inform children that they will be retelling the story before you read (Morrow 2015). • While listening, children who have advance notice of the upcoming retelling activity can analyze the story and plan what to include.
Introductions: Make them interactive	• Create interactive discussions with children through the use of questions (McGee 2008); model responses when necessary (Morrow 2015).

During Reading: Shared and Interactive Strategies

Reading the story for enjoyment the first time offers children a picture of the whole story as the author and illustrator intended. In the first read-aloud, teachers may stop once or twice to check in with children, but for the most part, the first reading is for pure enjoyment. When read to the whole class, the story becomes a shared class encounter—an experience from which all members of the classroom may draw. After the first read-aloud, shared reading, dialogic reading, and interactive read-aloud strategies are typically used as "during-reading" models while preparing for story retelling. All three models hold in common a theme of interaction. Sipe studied literacy practices in kindergarten and primary grade classrooms and (quite interestingly) found that over half (actually, close to two-thirds) of children's conversations about stories happened *during the reading* of the story—in which children sought out clarifications, made

To prepare for enacting the story, the teacher rereads the story to her troupe of actors. Discussion during reading helps children make clarifications.

speculations, wondered, performed, and interpreted the text (2008). Sipe concluded that "talking while the story unfolds is one of the unique affordances of the storybook read-aloud situation" (229). Not only is interaction a hallmark of the interactive read-aloud models used for story retelling, but interaction and teacher response are crucial to learning.

The Interactive Read-Aloud

An interactive read-aloud happens when teachers and children interact over a story that is read out loud to children. Interaction is purposeful and planned and includes children's questions and comments. It is conducted with a group of children who listen and respond to the reading of a story or nonfiction text. McGee reports that she uses whole-class read-alouds for the first reading of the story and moves to small-group formats for subsequent interactive readings (based on research demonstrating that young children's comprehension increases when working in small groups over whole-class or individual formats). "Small-group interactive read-alouds, followed by retelling or dramatizing, produce better results than interacting only with larger groups of children" (2008, 160). Working with small groups of children offers on-the-spot learning opportunities within meaningful literary conversations in highly motivating social contexts. Children may respond to the read-aloud by asking and answering questions, making comments, and suggesting predictions, for example. Teachers offer quality responses, expanding vocabulary and facilitating children toward higher skill levels in the midst of meaningful reading.

Dialogic Reading

Dialogic reading is a form of the interactive read-aloud strategy that was designed to increase children's expressive vocabulary by training adults in interactive book-reading strategies and selecting books for young children that are rich in vocabulary (Whitehurst et al. 1994). The method requires adults to introduce the book, ask questions while reading (avoiding yes, no, and where questions), and ask questions about the book after reading.

In dialogic reading, children's answers are always followed by adult responses. Adults are encouraged to repeat what children say. They acknowledge children's responses, offer elaboration, provide encouragement, and follow their interests. Adults are trained to ask open-ended questions and expand children's language. In Zevenbergen and Whitehurst's study, teachers and parents were encouraged to have fun. The researchers found a significant increase in immediate and long-term (six months postintervention) effects of expressive language among dialogic reading groups. Children participating in the intervention made significant vocabulary gains over the control group who were exposed to imaginative play activities instead of the dialogic reading intervention (2003).

Shared Reading

Shared reading is an interactive reading strategy similar to dialogic reading and interactive read-alouds. The presence of print and its focus in shared reading constitutes its primary difference. In interactive read-aloud and dialogic reading strategies, the printed story does not play a role. In shared reading, children and teachers "share" the reading experience together by relying on large print and pictures found in Big Books and chart paper. Children do not have to be readers to participate in shared reading. Shared reading is often used to draw attention to basic concepts of print, such as reading from left to right and top to bottom, making connections between the graphic (letter) and the phonemic (sound), and children's discovery of familiar words (such as the word *zoo*—known from exposure to environmental print—found in the word *zoom*). There is a focus on strong teacher support and scaffolding word-talk in a playful way: predicting words, sharing the reading together of repeated phrases in the story, and identifying letters, words, sentences, and punctuation as children develop. Shared reading offers opportunities for meaningful conversations about the mechanics of reading and provides a venue for inquiries in the context of sharing the reading together. Table 3.2 includes characteristics of all three read-aloud strategies used with preschool children.

Table 3.2: What Teachers Do: Approaches That Support Interaction During Reading

Strategy	Characteristic
Interactive read-alouds	• Includes quality before-, during-, and after-reading strategies. • During-reading is a context for vocabulary development and language/meaning expansions, asking and answering open-ended questions, making clarifications, predicting, wondering—which in repeated readings moves toward analysis dialogue. • Includes facilitating relatedness to the story and prompting children's responses. • McGee (2008) encourages whole-class first readings of the book and then small-group readings/interactions in subsequent readings. • Its hallmark is interactive analysis of text (vocabulary), characters, motivations, and predictions through teacher modeling and questioning. Children engage in actively predicting, making inferences, and asking and answering questions about the text while it is being read (during reading).
Dialogic reading	• Includes research-based, quality before-, during-, and after-reading strategies. • Includes facilitating relatedness to the story (making connections), prompting children's responses, asking open-ended questions, asking for predictions, and conducting multiple readings. • Encourages a family reading (with teacher modeling and enjoyment encouraged) as well as a school reading component. • Repeated readings of the book. • Strong response component with adults repeating children's verbal iterations, answering children's questions, and elaborating on children's answers. • Small-group interactive read-aloud strategies produce outcomes as opposed to large-group.
Shared reading	• Includes quality before-, during-, and after-reading strategies. • Focuses on the teacher facilitating a reading of the story to the group while pointing to the words (even when children can't read, they may participate in the shared reading experience) with a focus on accuracy of reading words. • Used with story retelling, interactions focus children on vocabulary, comprehension, sequence, or elements of story, for example. Teachers help children make connections to the story. They prompt children's responses and ask open-ended questions. • Teachers model reading with fluency and expression. In later readings: inclusion of children in reading repeated phrases or providing words as cloze-strategy. • Large print is needed for whole-class readings such as big books and large charts. • Materials are used to draw attention to problem-solving the print together: pointers, index cards, highlighters, and sticky notes.

After Reading: Story-Retelling Strategies

Similar to before- and during-reading experiences, teachers facilitate interaction about the text after reading. Teachers discern which strategies and emphasis areas to discuss with children after reading by gauging prior learning experiences with children's current responses to the text. Reviewing the text with children after reading appears as a key strategy that not only supports

One child looks for help from the teacher as she prompts the next part of *The Three Billy Goats Gruff*, enacted at the water table.

understanding of the story but also prepares for the child's story-retelling experience. In subsequent rereadings of the story, after-reading activities may focus more frequently on teacher modeling of story retelling with props, visual aids, or another mode (see Recommended Resources on organizing for story retelling in the back of this book). After-reading retellings move along a continuum from teacher-modeled to teacher-directed before scaffolding children toward independent group and individual practice in centers and during playtime.

As mentioned earlier, characteristics of what children do to acquire story-retelling proficiencies are identified by Dunst, Simkus, and Hamby in their meta-analysis (2012), as well as other sources (McGee 2008; Morrow 2015; Welsch 2008). Pivotal to setting children up for successful retellings are the following characteristics: adult coaching during practice, prompting during retellings, allowing for child elaborations, book access, dramatizations, visual aids, manipulatives (props), practice, and book-related pretend play. Of these, perhaps most is said about adult prompting.

Adult prompting appears as one of the common characteristics of child retellings among the studies in Dunst and colleagues' meta-analysis, providing insight into the need for teacher scaffolding while children are retelling stories (2012). Misconceptions about story retelling include the idea that young children should retell stories without practice, without help from others, or without props, when, in fact, research demonstrates that practice, scaffolding, and props are quite appropriate in assisting children toward the higher goal of language development and comprehending. "During retellings, teachers encourage children by prompting responses through scaffolding or modeling, asking questions, informing, and offering support for children's comments" (Morrow 1996, 267). Questions to facilitate story retelling with young children range from general prompts, such as "What happens next?" to more structured prompts needed for the child who is nonresponsive in story retelling.

Book-related pretend play supports and complements story-retelling goals. Why? Pretend play offers a context for learning in general, but it also serves as a venue for exploring and applying knowledge of story elements and structure in creative ways (Owocki 1999; Welsch 2008). Welsch moved her students from the predominantly media-related play she was observing in her preschool classroom toward literature-related play for the very reason of increasing comprehension. She defined "book-related pretend play" as follows:

> Student directed and initiated pretend play schemes and episodes in which students, through interactions with others, make object substitutions, integrate imaginary elements, or assume roles directly related to the characters, objects, actions, setting, language and themes found in children's literature. (2008, 139)

Welsch further made a case for not only *providing* children with story-related props, but also *introducing* the props to children, asking her preschoolers how the props could be used in the story before offering them for free and independent pretend play. Welsch's findings demonstrated that children indeed used the props to conduct play within and beyond the text. She analyzed themes in her observations that served as an organizational structure in her findings to note, for example, that children portrayed characters and expanded and extended story content. Welsch concludes that pretend play deepens book-related comprehension and serves as a viable observational venue for assessment.

Adding story-related props to free-play experiences, then following up with story-related facilitation, provides a supportive mechanism for children to deepen their understanding of the story and related vocabulary. Although Welsch's findings were limited to preschool, she suggests that book-related pretend play would nurture the love of reading and deepen comprehension goals for kindergarten and primary-grade students as well. Table 3.3 includes a summary of descriptors of after-reading teaching strategies.

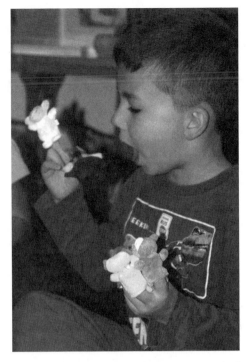

Exploration and playing with props is expected when young children begin story-retelling activities in either centers or small-group activities. Children additionally need access to props in free-play experiences.

Table 3.3: What Teachers Do: After-Reading Strategies

Strategy	Characteristic
Facilitate interaction	• Help children make connections (text-to-self connections with young learners especially). • Ask open-ended questions. • Ask higher-level questions (such as "Why do you think…?") to encourage inference, motivation, and other analysis (McGee and Schickedanz 2007).
Review the story with children	• Recall the story with children through questions, such as "What happened in the beginning of the story? After that?" • Reconstruct the story in sequence with children by asking questions and using picture cues as visual aids.

(continued on next page)

(continued from previous page)

Strategy	Characteristic
Teachers model story retelling	• Retell the story in your own words: use expression, dramatic pauses, and repeated phrases; present a model from which children may base their retellings. • Use props and/or visual aids (or another strategy, such as drawing or movement, for example); demonstrate how props or visual aids are effectively used in the retellings. • Specifically demonstrate or model how to use the retelling tools. • Use expression while retelling. • Change voices for different characters. • Make voice changes for key events if possible. • Use facial expressions. • Avoid being overly dramatic when retelling, as the drama will overtake the story.
Children practice story retelling with teacher support	• Provide coaching to children when they practice story retelling or book acting. • Support children with recalling the story as a group retell. • Prompt children while they retell stories when needed. • Encourage children to elaborate on specific parts of the story. • Provide children with access to books that are being retold and have the picture book available to serve as an aid for story retelling. • Include drama opportunities for retelling. • Facilitate a group reenactment of the story, with the teacher as director. • After modeling story retelling with props, distribute props to children and direct the group retelling with props. • Offer opportunities for children to work with props and other related materials, such as visual aids, for story retelling. • Organize the story into a structure or format to support children's successful retelling as needed. • Organize story-retelling centers for children to practice and receive teacher feedback. • Offer free play opportunities for story retelling.

Putting It All Together: Emphasizing Social Interaction During Read-Alouds

Quality interaction is integral to story-retelling teaching strategies; story retelling is all about communicating. Pinnell and Fountas, writing about early literacy practices in preschool settings, indicate that young children, especially those without many previous literacy experiences, "need to engage in conversation and storytelling to expand their oral language" (2011, 27). Most of the common characteristics in the meta-analysis of story retelling with young children by Dunst, Simkus, and Hamby are related to interaction (2012).

Common to quality early language and literacy development is the presence of social interaction and responsiveness either through repeating children's language, elaborating, providing feedback, or taking their language and understanding to a higher level (Vygotsky 1978; Morrow 1996; Bodrova and Leong 2006). Although language and literacy are truly embedded in books and various media-related resources, children's access to words and understanding is contingent on interaction, whether it is from a parent, a sibling, a caregiver, a peer, a teacher, or someone else. Teachers interact with children over narrative or expository text to promote expressive vocabulary development, facilitate children's understanding of the story, and encourage children to meet learning goals.

Quality interaction is crucial for developing language, comprehension, and understanding. "One of the goals for retelling is the reconstruction of story meaning through interactive discussions between adult and child" (Morrow 1996, 268). Children's understanding of what is and isn't important to story retelling comes from conversations about stories. In fact, it is the elimination of story-related interaction that produces the most limiting of consequences: memorizing, lack of understanding or comprehension, or filling in blanks or boxes on a page.

Story retelling with a peer and a copy of the book *Old MacDonald Had a Farm* resulted in rich interaction over which animal came next in this story-in-a-string retelling activity.

Social interaction helps children understand meanings and apply them as they experience life. Rosenblatt's transactional theory of reading holds that higher levels of textual understanding are acquired when a group can interact and exchange perspectives, transcending the individual understanding created from a single interpretation (1994). Literacy development thrives when teachers create classroom cultures that value interaction, inquiry, and oral and written language as part of their mini-lessons attached to reading stories. Providing audiences for children's retellings, whether through dramatizations, singing, or other strategies, is part of the social interaction component. Children can retell their stories to another group in the classroom, to a peer buddy, or in a pair-share scenario. To expand on the earlier descriptions of interaction as found in the three reading strategies, the next page has a more comprehensive list of responsive interactions when teaching for story retelling.

Interaction is core to the strategies used in building story-retelling skills in young children. Table 3.4: Interactive Teaching Strategies for Story Retelling is focused on interaction and its key strategies and characteristics.

Table 3.4 Interactive Teaching Strategies for Story Retelling

Strategy	Characteristic
Promote meaning through interaction	• Offer elaborative, meaning-focused interactions for increased vocabulary and comprehension. • Make the language of the text accessible to children. • Create child-friendly definitions to connect vocabulary, events, or problems in the story with children's lives. • Gather perspectives and encourage inquiries. • Prompt responses by asking children to comment or ask questions. • Model responses for children who are nonresponsive. • Engage children in active discussions.
Facilitate knowledge of story through interaction	• Ask children to make predictions. • Facilitate relatedness to the story (making connections); Morrow especially encourages text-to-self connections (1996; 2015). • Ask open-ended questions. • Facilitate construction (of story, meaning, sequence of events) and reconstruction. • Support recalling or summarizing. • Foster interpretation and perspective. • Encourage children to make comments, ask questions, and weigh in on teachers' and peers' questions and comments (McGee 2008). • Promote analysis by asking children why, to infer, to suggest character motivation.
Promote learning goals through interaction	• Encourage and provide feedback. • Acknowledge children's specific behaviors (rather than saying "good job"). • Respond to children's commentary; provide explanations as needed. • Offer positive affirmations. • Model responses if children cannot respond. • Reinforce positive attributes in story-retelling attempts. • Make connections between what children say and the story or retelling.

Designing Story-Retelling Experiences

Play is at the heart of learning. Teachers who understand how young children learn include elements of play in designing story retelling experiences as demonstrated in the props for *Mouse Count*, pictured (Walsh 1991). In many ways, simply using props for story retelling implies a playful experience. We offer children opportunities to begin small-group sessions by playing or exploring materials before facilitating them toward accuracy while retelling. Similarly, selecting literature, relevant materials, and developmental strategies to support children's retelling experiences are part of designing story-retelling activities. Teachers plan story-retelling experiences through a developmental perspective.

Planning with a Developmental Lens

Teachers develop children's understanding and skills by beginning where children currently are and move them toward deeper understandings. Children, as they grow, learn about things in their environment as they discover them in the real world—the concrete. As children develop further, they move toward more symbolic ways of understanding. They begin by symbolizing reality through pretending and playing with toys, called "action-based (enactive)," to higher levels of symbolizing using pictures, "image-based (iconic)," and finally to "language-based (symbolic)" (Bruner 1966, 11). Similarly, young children have a penchant for self-interest, so another continuum of learning is to move children away from self-interest toward an increased awareness of others' perspectives.

Young children learn by exploring, discovering, wondering, playing, and creating. Teachers must keep development in mind when finding enticing books and creating plans that align with how children learn.

Children's understandings and skills develop in patterns that are identified as "principles of developmental direction" (Kostelnik et al. 2015, 87). Essentially, the principles drive how we teach children so they learn deeper and more accurate concepts and skills:

- Known to unknown
- Simple to complex
- Self to other
- Whole to part
- Concrete to abstract
- Enactive to iconic to symbolic
- Exploratory to goal directed
- Less accurate to more accurate (Kostelnik et al. 2015, 87)

Principles of developmental direction affect how we plan effective story-retelling strategies and how children's retellings are assessed and analyzed (to facilitating their next steps in learning). When developing story-retelling experiences for young children, we combine our knowledge of how children learn with what we know about what works in story retelling. A picture book is composed of iconic (pictorial) and symbolic (printed word) representations of something concrete. When the teacher brought in props to help children enact *Mouse Count*, she bridged the iconic (pictures) and symbolic (words) in the book with a plastic jar, toy mice, and a plastic snake, something with which children could relate and enact—she was teaching with developmental principles in mind. She was teaching with play and, in the process, creating meaning through a story experience.

Children Learn through Exploration and Play

When children explore, they observe, manipulate, and test ideas or theories in an unrestrained manner. They gather information about the potentials and properties of the materials. Young children have a natural inclination to explore materials; exploration is essential to the learning process. Children are able to explore freely during open-ended, free-play experiences. Free play offers children an unconstrained time and space with materials while playing. Learning occurs from using and applying materials such as story-retelling props in creative and unrehearsed ways.

Exploring stories while engaged in free-play experiences is part of story retelling in preschool and kindergarten. While playing, children act out stories, create new endings, take on the role of a character, and make connections with themselves, the world, and other texts in creative ways. They say new words in risk-safe contexts. Children apply story-related concepts to other play scenarios or add a character to a real-life event while playing. Children use free play to explore concepts of story, characters, settings, and plot events and, in the process, deepen their understandings of vocabulary and the story itself (Owocki 1999, 2005; Welsch 2008). When literature-related props and materials are strategically placed in free-play areas, children use the materials to spark valuable literature explorations (Welsch 2008).

Although free play is a quality venue for imaginative play with literature-based materials and stories, guided play allows teachers to nurture children's need for play while they also learn (Weisberg, Hirsh-Pasek, and Golinkoff 2013).

The director of the preschool works with small groups of children in story retelling with the popular finger puppets in the library center.

Guided play is a teaching strategy that begins by capturing children's interests through materials or provocations (intentionally staged by the teacher), which naturally moves children toward exploration and play. In the case of story retelling, teachers facilitate children by exploring and playing with the props in small-group formats. Harnessing children's penchant for play, the teacher then guides children toward learning objectives by interjecting comments, encouraging reenactments or retellings of the story, using story-related vocabulary, and asking for explanations, clarifications, sequences, omissions, and so on. Each experience with the small group during the lifetime of the project lets the teacher guide learning in ways that scaffold or coach children while at the same time giving children ownership. Teachers set learning agendas, interact with children, and respond to children in ways that guide their learning through play-oriented work. They take children from exploration to goal-directed learning.

In story retelling, a guided play scenario often occurs in a library or puppet center with materials readily available to children. A teacher or paraprofessional works with small groups. Objectives for small-group work include teaching about props and character roles, reviewing key points of a story, directing small-group enactments with props or costumes, and revisiting the enactments or retellings through practice and more interaction. In guided play, teachers coach children toward accuracy, encourage vocabulary use, and respond to their approximations by leading them toward proficiency in retelling. Coaching nurtures children from less accurate retellings toward the accurate. Consistency helps children learn the rules of literature-based story retelling. One of the most important of these rules is to stick with the story so retellings move toward accuracy.

Selecting Interesting and Engaging Literature

When selecting books for an early retelling experience, teachers often start with simple, familiar texts and move toward more complex and unfamiliar stories. Literature selection for story retelling includes looking for stories with clear text, strong plot sequences, and vibrant characters. Books that include highly supportive illustrations offer children visual cues for comprehension. Teachers build story-retelling skills in very young students by engaging children in participative read-alouds, fingerplays, and pretend reading. Selecting interesting and engaging literature for early story retelling begins with the simple, familiar, and interactive as a way to support children in growing literacy skills and concepts.

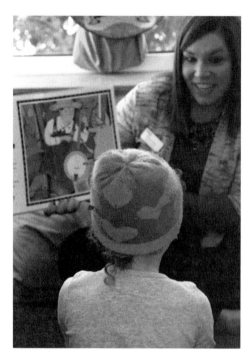

Selecting a book that tells the story of a familiar song, such as *Old MacDonald Had a Farm*, has a built-in component for successful story retelling and offers a good starting point for the young reteller.

Participative story experiences offer children early practice in skills needed for story retelling. Teachers using interactive story reading begin by teaching children responses to cues given while reading. Children learn to respond together and they learn to say or enact responses when cued by practicing with the teacher. Because it is a participative and enjoyable group experience, the interactive experience is psychologically safe and less stressful than individual performance-based retelling. Participative stories offer teachers a way to begin (and continue) to develop the skills of expression, sound effects, voice, and body language for story retelling. Examples of interactive, participative reading strategies include asking children to roar when the lions appear, to make rain sounds by rapidly tapping their hands on their knees when we reach a certain page, or to echo repetitive phrases in the book.

Books such as *We're Going on a Bear Hunt* are designed for interactive reading and listening experiences with young children (Rosen 1997). Robert Munsch, author and storyteller, encourages teachers and caregivers to expand their conceptions of interactive reading toward thinking of ways to create participation in stories. Stories that are not call-and-response or interactive from the start may become interactive for children if teachers make them so. Munsch encourages teachers to put interaction back into stories by creating "participation elements, verbal games, rhythmic chanting, slapping, and imitation" and "repetitive patterns" (Munsch 1994, 33).

Fingerplays are another example of interactive story retelling, as are songs and rhymes. Fingerplays mix a story, song, or rhyme with the physical action of using one's fingers to represent characters or objects. Teachers can supplement fingerplays by creating finger or glove puppets with simple materials that can enhance number concepts in the process.

When prereaders pretend to read a book after having it read to them, teachers learn about what children understand about books, reading, and story: Do they hold the book right-side up? Do they include details in the text? Do they borrow words from the text? We can also make some hypotheses about what they remember and understand about the book. Teachers ask questions at the end of pretend reading to clarify. Pretend reading is a form of story retelling worth documenting and analyzing, especially if it is all pretend and none of it makes sense. The child is pretending to read!

Wordless picture books offer potential to support story retelling. Any book can be modeled by a teacher and pretend read or retold by a child, but quality wordless picture books offer highly effective illustrations because the pictures are the only means for telling the story. Wordless picture books have value for beginning story retellers if teachers model how to read one and collaboratively retell the story with children. The key is in telling the stories in your own words, using rich vocabulary, interacting in the process, and developing understanding. Often teachers write out a story frame on sticky notes for each double-page spread in advance of reading a wordless book. In Eric Carle's nearly wordless book *Do You Want to Be My Friend?*, Carle offers a sample text to get us started in the front matter of the book (1976). Wordless picture books serve as inspiration for a great play often directed by the preschool teacher. *A Ball for Daisy*, Chris Raschka's beloved wordless Caldecott Award winner, requires a couple of pretend dogs, two pretend owners, and a pair of pretend balls (2011).

High-quality pictures help children un-

A book based on a fingerplay that children are learning in school encourages interaction while reading. In this case, *Pete the Cat: Five Little Pumpkins* (Dean 2015) offers children spontaneous informal readings and interactions during centers time.

Children explore props and practice scenes before enacting *A Ball for Daisy*, whose themes of making new friends, loss of a favorite toy (a ball), and finally restitution lend toward enactments because so many emotions are part of the book.

derstand meaning and sequence and support vocabulary development. Often, illustrations move beyond the text, and teachers shouldn't be surprised when children add story-retelling details found in pictures that are not included in the text. Teachers are very word-focused—understandably so when they are teaching children how to read. Children, on the other hand, are naturally drawn to visual images, which offer enhanced meanings to words. Illustrations depicting vocabulary, plot, and characters support children in comprehending. Once children are able to read independently with accurate comprehension, pictures become less important. We begin by selecting books with heavily supportive illustrations for early retellers and move toward worrying less about the illustrations with children who are proficient readers.

Playful story retelling with older infants and young toddlers might begin with enacting the simple language in a familiar concept book about balls or interacting over the simple text in *No, David!* (Shannon 1998). A next step in early story-retelling experiences might be a board book of the song *Itsy Bitsy Spider* read, sung, and enacted together with the child using props. Again, moving toward the familiar add-on book, *Brown Bear, Brown Bear, What Do You See?*, coupled with props or visual aids may offer a built-in structure for story retelling with strong repetitive text. The more complex *Three Bears* or *Three Little Pigs* may serve as a next step for preschoolers with their repetitive texts and plot structures. Coupled with teacher guidance, coaching, supportive structures, props, and enacting, retelling a story with repetitive sections can be a successful and intellectual experience. The process of learning story retelling provides opportunities for analyzing stories and getting at meaning through practice sessions and interaction. Teachers gauge movement toward a more difficult and less familiar story with children as they scaffold toward children's learning and developmental needs.

Scaffolding children toward success in story retelling by moving from simple books to complex text selections doesn't mean, however, that we should refrain from offering complexity in story retellings to children. I've observed grand, orchestrated group retellings and dramatizations of very complex stories in preschool—what McGee calls "book acting" (2008, 157). In these cases, teachers act as directors of plays and offer children strong scaffolding, narration, direction, and opportunities to dramatize the book with props. Indeed, doing so offers potential for growth in vocabulary, working together, and building community. Teachers counter the more complex story with mediation and involvement in the retelling.

Choosing Materials

Storytellers use various strategies to help them remember stories. A second grader may rely on visualizing a map of the story to organize the parts of the story into the whole while retelling. Alternatively, a preschool teacher may create a story path on laminated butcher paper, filled with visual cues for her young learners to follow while retelling. Perhaps the reteller selected a story that has three of something, such as bears or pigs, and likewise the very structure of the story helps her remember. Whereas a first grader might remember by touching a story-retelling bracelet with a yellow bead to represent a house of straw, a brown bead to represent a house of sticks, and a red bead to represent a house of brick, a preschooler may need a finger puppet representative of each of the three houses for retelling. Maybe the story has repeating phrases, such as "This porridge is too hot," "too cold," "just right!"; or "The wolf huffed and he puffed . . . ," a story pattern often found in traditional tales and other books written specifically for young children. If so, the storyteller keeps track of each segment of the story and uses the repeating phrase to transition to the next segment. Teachers choose materials as props to support children with story

A mixture of puppets and toys serve as props for a favorite version of *Little Rabbit Foo Foo* (Rosen and Robbins 1993). This story may be retold using just the two main recurring characters. With multiple props, teachers may engage large groups by giving each child a role to play (and prop to hold) when modeling story retelling after reading.

elements such as characters or settings. They use maps or shapes or other materials to support children with organizing the structure of story.

Organizing stories means that we add a component to the materials that helps young children remember the story. It serves as a visual reminder of the sequence or key components. A striped page of colors may prompt children in knowing what comes next in *Brown Bear*. One teacher made a story-retelling path on large butcher paper. As the child walked down the path, he'd notice rocks with picture clues about characters, plot, problems, and solutions. The Recommended Resources section includes typical structures for story retelling. When teachers create an organizational structure for retelling (such as a story on a string or paint-stirring stick for add-on or counting stories), they model it and use it with children and encourage children to use it when they choose story-retelling centers-based work on their own. Organizing stories for children through such methods assists children in successful story retelling while implicitly teaching concepts of story structure.

Props are materials such as blankets, toys, and puppets that serve to assist children in story retelling and remembering. When children have an opportunity to learn from concrete materials through exploration and observation, they are learning through an authentic experience—particularly helpful with young children. Props, when used with story retelling, help children remember key story elements and plot sequences.

The continuum of enactive to iconic to symbolic representation is related to using story-retelling materials with children (Bruner 1966). When props are authentic and real, such as a branch or a sunflower, they are considered as concrete materials. Children who pretend or enact scenarios with props are using enactive levels of representation to express themselves and relate to objects while developing understanding. At a further symbolic representational level, visual aids—pictures applied to card stock, blocks, or boxes, for example—scaffold children's story-retelling prowess by offering cues as reminders of the story or nonfiction narrative. Using beads in the place of props or pictures is more symbolic still. Children are required to remember more on their own and rely more heavily on language while retelling. The next level is to use only words with no props. Core to story retelling with young children, props, and visual aids (and symbols such as beads) serve a scaffolding role. They support understanding the complexities of story: its internal structure or rules that define what story is (the concept of story), the nuances of this particular story, its repeated phrases, and expressions and drama where needed.

As children develop and learn new concepts, whether they are infants and toddlers or second graders, it is beneficial to offer the real thing if possible. The concept of moving from the concrete to the abstract learning experience is not limited to teaching young children. When I taught a group of early childhood educators learning about outdoor education, we borrowed natural history trunks from a local university (they lend teaching trunks to educators at low or no cost). The teaching trunks offered us amazing experiences with handling feathers, nests, rocks, minerals, and dinosaur bones and teeth.

Models or children's toys offer teachers the next-best thing to reality. Stories and nonfiction literature are explored, clarified, retold, and/or enacted using toys, puppets, or models. Authentic models offer teaching and learning opportunities when the real thing is not available: models of eyes are taken apart and put together, for example, when learning about the sense of sight. Toys give children a method of enacting story retelling through something that isn't real but looks like the real thing.

Moving up the symbolic ladder, icons (pictures) serve as visual aids in story retelling with young children. Cut illustrations out of old, used copies of books, back them with construction paper or card stock, then add lamination or contact paper coverings. Mrs. Whitmore, a preschool teacher in a mixed Head Start, Title-One, and district pre-K inclusive classroom, places her simple *Brown Bear* icons (cutouts from a die-cut machine) on wooden blocks that stand in sequence to serve as icons as the story is retold.

By cutting out five small pumpkins from a paper plate, laminating them, and adding a Velcro dot to each, a simple glove puppet is created for young children to use in retelling *Pete the Cat: Five Little Pumpkins.*

Whether using concrete materials, props or toys, pictures laminated on blocks, or colored beads to represent events in a story, the use of story-retelling materials is integral in both learning about story retelling and creating meaning. Props, visual aids, and organizing structures serve as "remembrances" or scaffolds or prompts to retelling the story and support vocabulary development in young children.

Using props from early story-retelling experiences onward, whether using a blanket in a game of peek-a-boo or star-gazer lilies to explore the ways bees find pollen in flowers, is based on young learners' developmental needs. We don't only use concrete materials with infants and toddlers and end with symbolic materials in third grade. Instead, our use of concrete materials is strategic and meaningful for all ages. The concrete item may be observed, explored, and revisited to test hypotheses. The most engaging of early childhood classrooms have inquiry-inducing science and social studies centers (accompanied by real materials, nonfiction books, and inquisitive children).

Children Advance through Scaffolding

Scaffolding is a process of mediating information to make it accessible to children so they are able to understand and learn. Bruner coined the word "scaffolding" to describe Vygotsky's concept of social mediation in learning—using collaboration, interactive support, language, and other tools (such as modeling, templates, props, or visual aids in story retelling, or manipulatives, for example, in counting)—to help others move from what they know to their next levels in development (Wood, Bruner, and Ross 1976, 90). Scaffolding is a key strategy in teaching and learning. Scaffolding requires the use of language, and with young children, scaffolding includes the use of concrete materials, props, or visual aids. Scaffolding includes explanations, demonstrations, modeling, telling, guiding, or coaching a child along the learning path.

When scaffolding information for children, we begin where children are in their current understandings—the known. Teachers move from heavy support and assistance toward lighter support and assistance during the story-retelling process. How much teacher support is offered depends on several variables: the complexity of the book, the role required of the child, and the responsiveness of the child. Teacher support may appear (to the outsider) as heavy through the end of the experience (as in the case of preschool children acting out Marcia Brown's *Stone Soup* with teacher direction), but support at the end is less than at the beginning of the experience.

Coaching is one way of scaffolding children in their retellings. It moves young children toward awareness that the book is a story-model, and although there are many different ways to retell, the essence of the story remains the same. Although the story may take on many forms in free play, the child learns, through coaching, that our story-retelling learning needs are to stick with the story and retell it similarly to how the author shared it with us. For the sake of creativity, I hope teachers will be adamant about offering story props during free-play time for continued exploring and imaginings.

One teacher of a district-run preschool uses complex stories representative of the cultures of children in the classroom to make challenging language, complexity of story, and culture more accessible to children through story acting. She is able to use complex stories because she takes on the role of director of the play and continuously narrates and provides directions and cues

This teacher coaches a child on his lines before their first group retelling during small-group time.

to children. Her scaffolding at the beginning of the story-retelling process, however, was much heavier than at the end when children knew their roles in the enactments. Although she was still heavily supporting the process at the end with narration, directions, and cues to children, it was less supportive than in the beginning when she was helping them discover what to say, make props, and know when to speak and where to stand. Because of the story's complexity, children performed at levels of assistance rather than at independent levels at the end of the project. The language exposure was simply supreme as the story was practiced, analyzed, and discussed many times before the enactment (to families). The more experiences children have with story retelling, the more able they are to take on greater responsibility.

Teachers Use the Creative Arts to Support Learning and Expressing

In early childhood and beyond, the creative arts serve as a way for teachers to observe and learn about children's development in all domains of learning. While children interact with each other when building a three-dimensional structure, we collect data on social and emotional behavior. We get a picture of their dexterity and problem-solving processes as they negotiate building with each other. When children mimic animal movements, we capture data about their gross motor functioning. We gather information on their conceptualizations of specific animals by observing their movements and asking them questions. While children

The teacher leads children in creating a bear out of colored dough. Dough bears will dry and be used as props for their next retelling of *Goldilocks and the Three Bears*.

draw pictures, we obtain information about their fine motor skills and range of development in drawing. We capture information about their conceptualizations by asking questions. When children use two sticks to create a rhythm or they sing or play a keyboard, we acquire information about their use of pattern and ability to reproduce music or song in either a standard or creative way. When children pretend to make dinner and go to the store, they are acting out events that are important in their lives. They use language, planning, negotiating, and invented or authentic stories to create their dramatic play. The creative arts include primary disciplines of music, the dramatic arts, movement, and the visual arts—each viable ways to tell stories.

Experiential and symbolic, the creative arts—coupled with a capable guide or teacher—serve as a powerful venue for learning, and they deepen children's understanding. They allow children to explore properties of color, clay, and other materials. The creative arts offer opportunities to symbolize an eye with a button when making a collage. In early childhood, the creative arts serve as a means for revisiting, reconstructing, and communicating or, rather, retelling stories. Using a guided play format for working in small groups, children and their teachers explore the story and make plans:

- How will we pretend to be the people in the book (the characters)? Will we use the story props and tell the story? Act the story out?

- What does it mean when "Max hammered out a reply on the cans, *Cling . . . clang . . . da-BANG!*"? (Support discussions about the definition with a hammer to share and try out, then drumsticks, comparing sounds.) What does "hammered" mean? What sound does "hammered" make? Use two sticks from outdoors like Max had, or use rhythm sticks. (While reading *Max Found Two Sticks*, Pinkney 1997, 22.)

- May we let "little blue" and "little yellow" sing a short song of sadness when their tears are falling? What might they sing? What words will they use while they're singing? How might you sound when you're sad? (While reading *Little Blue and Little Yellow*, Lionni 1995.)

- How would an elephant move? Will you show us?

Using the creative arts with guided-play teaching strategies in story-retelling centers offers children ways to playfully explore concepts of story, elaborate on word meanings, and create rhythms or songs to communicate mood, expression, or dialogue. We offer visualizations of characters through art, masks, illustration, or costuming. We imagine and construct settings. We *become* the story, and as a result, we understand.

The creative arts give us an opportunity to explore the whole story and examine its parts. Expression through the arts requires examination and analysis because we are compelled to create and represent a portion of the story with accuracy. When we prepare for retelling, we consider the big question—what

A Box Can Be Many Things encourages dramatic story retelling and later inspires creative play (Rau 1997). By enacting the story first, then moving the worn-out box to the house center, the flattened box became a bed for the sleepy dad while Mom and Teacher took care of the baby.

was the story about?—and then consider the parts that make up the whole. Story retelling requires us to analyze the parts—the essence of the character, the hallmark of the setting, the core of the problem, the joy of the solution—and how we reconstruct, represent, and communicate these parts of the story to others.

When planning for story-retelling experiences with young children, teachers use the creative arts during guided play in three primary ways: (1) to promote meaning—through using vocabulary words and applying story elements with accuracy; (2) to encourage creative expression—by problem solving, negotiation, analysis, and interaction; and (3) to stimulate communication—using speaking, sound effects, props, drama, music, or dance. By embracing the creative arts as part of the story-retelling process, children benefit from the many ways of analyzing, expressing, and revisiting story.

Teachers Plan Retelling and Enacting with Audiences

Denise Fleming's books are marked with powerful verbs coupled with highly creative artwork (she paints with colored pulp using squeeze bottles and trays or frames). She uses words to express actions because she wants her books to inspire people to act them out. She believes "picture books are like small plays" (Fleming in Reading Rockets, n.d.). In classrooms with preschool children, teachers orchestrate small-group practice sessions that later lead toward retelling or book acting to another small group or the whole class. As children gain experience and maturity, they are paired with a classmate or use group sharing time for the purpose of retelling and listening to stories.

Young children are by nature self-oriented. They likely are more concerned with their own stories and retellings than listening to others'. But story retelling encourages the teller (the self) to think of the listener (the other). For young children, this experience not only supports developing a concept of what it takes to communicate with others in general, but also the development of understanding of the story within oneself and how that understanding is communicated effectively to the "other" for similar understandings. In the presence of the audience, communication skills are built. The child is now concerned with questions such as "Did you understand? What was missing from the story that made you not understand?"

Part of the overall structuring of retelling in the environment is to understand that the more the story is oriented to the known, self, big picture or whole, concrete, enactive, exploratory, and less accurate, the more teachers will be simplifying story-retelling experiences for young children. Alternatively, the more oriented toward the unknown, other, details or parts, abstract, symbolic, goal directed, and more accurate, the more likely teachers will create a complex environment for story retelling (Kostelnik et al. 2015, 91). Designing story-retelling experiences entails weaving principles of developmental direction with components of planning: selecting stories, identifying vocabulary, planning read-alouds, harnessing play, choosing materials, scaffolding learning, using the creative arts, and including audiences.

Part 2

Weaving Story Retelling into the Curriculum

Part of the magic of story retelling with young children is found in "becoming" the story. Whether we enact or retell, sing or create, the story becomes part of the young child just as the child becomes the story.

Annie Lionni shared about her grandfather's creative process:

Leo would quote a book that he read years ago—"When a painter paints a tree, he becomes a tree." Whatever we create, he believed, we fill in with our own thoughts and feelings. . . . But when Leo said he became a tree, he also thought that the tree became him. "Of course, I am Frederick," he said, referring to one of my favorite characters, Frederick the Mouse. And he was Swimmy when he became the eye of the giant fish. (2007, 50)

Children appear to have an innate ability to simply lose themselves in play. Teachers harness play for the benefit of reaching learning goals when we coach children in retelling stories, such as encouraging children to apply story-related vocabulary words, remember to include the problem, and follow up with providing the solution. Story-retelling learning goals reach beyond the story, however, and into the area of content or disciplinary-related objectives when we include story retelling as a strategy for applying STEM, number sense, or social and emotional concepts, for example. In part 2, we'll set the stage for "becoming" the story and applying content-area vocabulary when we integrate story-retelling strategies across the curriculum so the story might "become" us.

Building Social and Emotional Concepts with Story Retelling

Story retelling serves as a strategy for children to experience a common story, enact and retell it, and learn about social and emotional concepts in the process. Through interactive teaching, children delve more deeply into stories by focusing on basic word meanings, sharing what is happening, and making connections to their own lives. Stories and retelling strategies offer children the vocabulary of responding to others, coping methods, and social skills that may serve as options from which children can draw when in authentically stressful situations. Picture books have the advantage of art or photographs that model these concepts, such as in *Say Hello!*, a delightful book that uses simplistic, brightly colored illustrations to explore the concept of greeting others in socially acceptable ways (Davick 2015).

Defining Social-Emotional Learning Goals

Emotional and social learning are two separate but interdependent domains. Related fields such as child guidance, creative problem solving, and approaches to learning are often discussed in the social and emotional domains. A brief exploration of terms will help reveal definitions necessary for designing meaningful learning experiences for children.

Morning rituals offer a structure for building community through beginning with saying hello in different ways. Literature-based story retelling is one strategy in developing social and emotional concepts and strategies in children.

The Emotional Domain

Facilitating understanding within the emotional domain often begins with recognizing and labeling feelings in oneself as well as learning how to manage those feelings. Head Start goals for young children include recognizing emotions in self and others as part of "emotional functioning" (2015). Typically, our starting point in working with young children is labeling feelings. A concerned

Using the book and built-in props for *Glad Monster, Sad Monster*, this teacher reads the story to children. She prompts children while reading, using open-ended questions. She models using the props before giving them to children, and she facilitates them in making faces to match emotions.

parent or caregiver may pick up a crying newborn and cuddle her to soothe her (an act of compassion), and begin the process of labeling this emotion by saying, "You are so sad, little one; what's wrong?" Although the child is a newborn, the parents' and caregivers' repeated efforts of providing labels, using an empathetic tone of voice, offering compassionate action, and continued guidance throughout childhood nurture this baby toward awareness of her own feelings as she grows older.

After children have a chance to relish and enjoy a good book for the first time, some books, such as *Show Me Happy*, ask children to get up and "show me giving" and "show me sharing when we play" (Allen 2015). No props needed! Other books that focus on labeling emotions, such as the classic *Glad Monster, Sad Monster* are so primed for props that the author and illustrator provide them to the reader in the book (Emberley and Miranda 1997). It is actually difficult to read the book without using the props!

The development of self-awareness flows from the child developing a working understanding of emotions. A self-aware child is able to understand how emotions affect behavior (CASEL 2013). As children learn to interact with others, they develop a sense of "self-identity" (Head Start 2015). When children develop concepts of themselves, they gain the following ideas:

- I am a unique individual with my own abilities, characteristics, emotions, and interests.
- I have confidence in my own skills and positive feelings about myself.

Books that promote self-awareness and self-identity are typically a lot of fun for children to explore. *Tacky the Penguin* continues to withstand the test of time and remains a favorite among young children, likely due to Tacky's comfort level with his own individuality and offbeat behavior (Lester 1988). It is a book with a real problem that gets resolved, and for this reason alone, it is a good one to read with young children. In *Harold Finds a Voice*, the main character, Harold, is a parrot who can be the voice of many things: alarm clock, coffeepot, cell phone, toaster, blender, TV set, and so on. When he is brave enough to try out his own voice, however, he is at first quite disappointed with the sound of it: "*rawk.*" Soon Harold finds out that his awful-sounding voice drew a flock of bird friends just like him. By the end, Harold comes to terms with his own voice and, in essence, his self-identity (Dicmas 2013). Harold's story is much like many self-identity discovery and acceptance stories. The problem is typically that of the main character disliking something about himself, but eventually he comes to appreciate that singular, self-defining characteristic that makes him unique. A parallel pattern of self-identity books often has a young animal either trying out the sounds or physical components of other animals until this animal discovers or comes to terms with self-identity, such as in *The Mixed-Up Chameleon*, in which, after becoming a hilarious composite of everything he saw at the zoo, the mixed-up chameleon finally says at the end of the book, "I wish I could be myself"—which of course is granted (Carle 1974).

The Social Domain

The social domain requires a more sophisticated blending of emotional knowledge, skills, and dispositions. Social awareness, for example, is often defined as respecting and understanding others' perspectives. The idea of "other" in these definitions is typically inclusive of those whose cultures, races, and past experiences differ from our own. Gartrell indicates that growth in "accepting unique human qualities in others" is a democratic life skill (he identifies five democratic life skills) intentionally cultivated through teacher guidance (2012, 135). One children's book that shows the importance of understanding others' perspectives is Klassen's *This Is Not My Hat* (2012). While the small fish who stole a bowler hat from a very large, sleeping fish rationalizes his perspective in his escape route, the larger victim of the theft has his own perspective of the situation.

Children most effectively gain social-emotional skills in the context of interaction. Epstein, however, indicates that interaction with peers and adults is not quite enough: children need quality "child guided experiences" to develop the ability to empathize with the feelings of others (2014, 2). When teachers and others help children grow their concepts of empathy toward understanding and acting on their powers to share, care, and help others, children are nurtured in compassion and grow into warmhearted individuals (Copple and Bredekamp 2009). *A Sick Day for Amos McGee* is a delightful book choice relating to compassion. The story is about a dedicated zookeeper whose animal friends take care of him when he is ill (Stead 2010).

Developing friendships, relationships, and being part of a group are another level of social-emotional development. Belonging is connected to self-identity and, indeed, security in one's own skills, awareness of one's feelings about self, and understanding of one's own uniqueness (Head Start 2015). Belonging is inclusive of family groups, community groups, and others. Friendships, relationships, and belonging inevitably require social skills such as noticing and responding to others' interactions, needs, and interest levels. In addition, the child must be able to communicate effectively with others, employ active listening skills, work with others, negotiate with others, ask for help or provide assistance, and make ethical decisions (CASEL 2013). Again, in this arena, "interpreting human differences" or "accepting unique human qualities in others" assists in developing relationships and group membership (Gartrell 2012, 135–36). *Friendshape,* by Amy Krouse Rosenthal and Tom Lichtenheld, offers characteristics of friendships in a simple concept book format (2015).

Making friends and belonging are supported by classroom norms or rules that hold at their foundation safety and respect. These can be as simple as "we take care of ourselves, each other, and our things." Children's books that draw out characteristics of friendship support a classroom culture of caring and belonging.

In essence, an ultimate goal of developing responsible decision making in young children requires teachers to guide children toward working understandings of fairness, safety, respect, ethics, and compassion. Problem solving is part of responsible decision making. Modeling decision-making processes (think-out-loud strategies, for example) helps children understand what making responsible decisions entails.

The reality of social-emotional development is that we are developing in both domains at the same time. Children therefore need scaffolding and guidance from teachers and other adults (Epstein 2009, 2014; Gartrell 2012). Nurturing children's knowledge, skills, and dispositions toward social and emotional competence is at the forefront of our work with young children. It reasonably might be argued that stories and retelling were the original social-emotional curriculum—perhaps since the dawn of human language and communication.

Organizing for Social-Emotional Development through Story Retelling

Current thinking about how teachers impact young children's social and emotional development is essentially categorized in three broad areas: social interaction, environments, and curriculum (Epstein 2014; CSEFEL 2006). As discussed in earlier chapters, each area is essential not only for developing story retelling, but also in facilitating social and emotional learning skills and strategies.

Social Interaction

Just as teacher interactions affect early literacy skills, vocabulary, and concept development, interactions also strengthen growth and development in the social and emotional domains. The ways teachers respond to and guide children in the context of their social situations have tremendous impact. Children in the midst of their own social-emotional successes and concerns are more likely to learn from immediate positive feedback, guidance, and support from teachers, parents, and caregivers. Epstein offers three key ways teachers may facilitate social-emotional learning with young children through interaction:

- modeling
- coaching
- providing opportunities for practice (2014, 45–46)

Story retelling does all three.

As children develop social and emotional skills, they constantly make adjustments as a result of their social-play experiences. We want children to learn the pleasures of positive social interaction and belonging. Interaction is the authentic educator of social-emotional learning. When teachers are offering modeling in the context of social interaction, they can draw on a relevant story and retelling or enacting experience as a resource. Whether children are engaged in free play or group learning, direct instruction or discovery, social interaction or isolative play behavior, we know that positive classroom environments are the places for trying out social and emotional skills and knowledge.

Environments

The classroom environment can be considered in two ways: as a physical place with furniture, materials, and equipment for teaching and learning; and as a psychological setting for nurturing and guiding growth and social and emotional development. In early childhood settings, we welcome and value children and their families' cultures and include respectfulness and learning about ourselves and others as part of our classroom environment. In such settings, children learn how to interact as a group member. They learn how to respect multiple perspectives and diversity among members of a community. Children learn respect for cultural practices different from their own. When children listen to new ideas, consider alternative perspectives, and try different food choices, they widen their perspectives and broaden their understandings (with guidance in these areas from their caregivers, teachers, and parents). Young children need environments that are both physically and psychologically safe to healthily develop in emotional and social domains. In addition to safety, a positive, responsive, and supportive classroom environment contributes greatly to social-emotional development.

In early childhood classrooms, teachers create the physical environment of a classroom to meet developmental needs of their young learners. Children need materials to manipulate, explore, observe, and play. Inspired by the work of educators in Reggio Emilia, Curtis and Carter go further and offer ideas about provocations for inquiry and exploration (2003). They challenge teachers to consider aesthetics and create beautiful spaces and homelike environments, and they encourage the use of natural materials to educate young children. Children also need opportunities to choose materials, work and play in small groups, and seek alone time. So they might grow in self-efficacy, children need opportunities to self-direct. They also need guidance from teachers about boundaries.

Just as children need physically safe and stimulating environments, they need psychologically safe and nurturing environments as well. According to Erikson, psychosocial development is contingent on how children meet challenges as they grow into adulthood and onward. Erikson believed that the toddler years are when children develop a sense of autonomy that supports the child as he or she develops self-efficacy. Per Erikson, we continue (or choose not to continue) to revisit the status of autonomy within us as we grow and develop, and we have opportunities to develop further into more (or less) autonomous individuals. If very young children are in an environment that is discouraging or constricted, if they hear "no" too often and have few opportunities to make choices, Erikson believed that very young children would develop shame or doubt instead of autonomy (1993).

Similarly, in the preschool years, children learn to take initiative. Children develop initiative when teachers support and encourage them to choose, make plans, and carry out their plans in realistic ways. Alternatively, if few or no opportunities to create plans and carry them out are offered to children, they will become frustrated or they may make bad decisions. Because they have the desire to take initiative and cannot, they may develop feelings of guilt. When classrooms provide psychological safety, children feel safe to take social and cognitive risks, make choices, develop autonomy, and take initiative—all necessary in learning deeper and more difficult concepts and skills later on.

Story retelling gives children an opportunity to take initiative and become a character in a play or retell an entire story. Environments supportive of social-emotional development provide children with developmentally appropriate story-retelling books with social-emotional themes, complete with props or visual aids from which children may select. Children may choose to enact or retell the story with a friend—or perhaps they will take the story and materials to the block center for a new adventure or free-play invention of new story twists or a new ending. Whatever the case, providing children with story-retelling books, props, and materials in the environment extends curriculum and builds autonomy and initiative.

Curriculum

Teachers are increasingly aware that just as children need curriculum in cognitive learning, they also need curriculum in social and emotional learning. Similarly, just as language is a tool for teaching math and science concepts, the language of social-emotional literacy is very important. Literature-based story retelling and enacting are ways to practice social-emotional concepts and skills in a safe, nonpersonal experience. Role playing is a key strategy used both by teachers of young children and psychologists when counseling children and families in social and emotional areas. When we merge the dramatic arts, puppets, or other props as a way to reenact or retell a story with a social-emotional focus, we are offering children ways to recognize and understand feelings, discover and practice positive interactions, learn and rehearse coping strategies, and recognize and celebrate self-efficacy.

Organizing story retelling in social and emotional curriculum involves finding books that address themes and topics in social and emotional domains. Reading the needs of children, then finding books that meet those needs, is one of the most effective ways to offer children a social-emotional learning experience through a story. Retelling or enacting a story requires children to "try on" the characters and their coping strategies, relationship skills, problem-solving strategies, and decision-making skills. It allows teachers to draw from story-retelling experiences and resources to apply to an authentic social situation. One of the reasons stories appeal to us is that the words we read or hear resonate within us. Story holds potential to change our thinking, to increase our understanding, and to strengthen our convictions. We're hooked to stories because we love learning more about ourselves and others' interpretations of human nature.

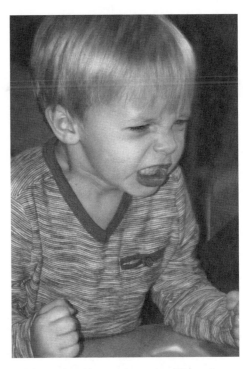

While reading, the teacher asks children to create facial expressions that depict specific emotions. Doing so helps children label their own and others' emotions while also supporting skills needed for effective story retelling and communicating in general.

Story retelling gives children opportunities to revisit social and emotional learning situations posed in stories. Reading stories together allows children a commonly shared experience; children's literature provides a medium for addressing and developing concepts with children in just about any topic. Most of our picture books touch on social and emotional themes. We worry over Goldilocks when she enters the bear family home, and we empathize with Baby Bear who feels violated over his stolen porridge, broken chair, and occupied bed. Goldilocks did not respect others' things—a social concept. Yet this book is typically not considered an obvious choice for social-emotional retelling.

The potentials of using story retelling as a curricular strategy for developing children's social-emotional learning are limited only by the imagination. In the following section of this chapter, we use social-emotional big ideas to guide selection of literature and experiences to facilitate social-emotional growth and development. While using these activities, plan for interactive read-alouds and model story retelling with children:

- Read with enjoyment in the first reading (often as a whole class).

- Revisit the story over time (often in small groups) to develop depth of understanding by focusing on key features and skills to support retelling, such as vocabulary development, comprehension, identifying the problem, characters, and so on.

- Move toward modeling story retelling or enactments in after-reading experiences (both whole class and small groups as appropriate).

- Encourage, support, and scaffold small-group story-retelling practice sessions; consider small-group guided play as an optimal way of supporting story retelling.

- Include props in free-play centers.

Enactments and retelling with puppets and other props help children get into their roles for social-emotional concept development. In the following section, sample books, props, and suggestions provide a starting point for weaving story retelling into social-emotional curriculum.

Story Retellings for Supporting Social and Emotional Learning

Sense of Identity and Appreciating Difference

P. Zonka Lays an Egg by Julie Paschkis (2015)

Paper plates folded in half transform into hen and rooster characters with the use of watercolor paints, markers, and construction paper. Adding a basket of plastic eggs completes the props for a group retelling or enactment or as an activity in a center when the study has ended.

Summary of the Story	Why This Book Has Potential for Story Retelling
P. Zonka, a chicken, has difficulty laying eggs because she was so distracted with springtime nature observations, she just hasn't tried. P. Zonka's name is inspired by the Ukrainian decorated egg, *pysanka*, so when she does lay an egg, it is a Ukrainian decorated egg.	The story has a problem, though it is a small one: P. Zonka doesn't lay eggs. The problem is resolved when she is encouraged to try. The inclusion of four chickens, one rooster, and four eggs make the story fairly simple for young children to enact with easy-to-make props.

Vocabulary		Relationship Strategies Addressed in the Story
• rooster	• dandelion	• Trying, which is sometimes very difficult, can help you do something even if you don't think (or no one else thinks) you can.
• chicken	• midnight	
• crow (as in "cock-a-doodle-do")	• lazy	• Focusing on the task can help you try and help you succeed.
• staring	• nervous	
• gawking	• cackle	• Find the uniqueness and beauty in yourself and others.
• dreamer	• fluffed	
• gazed	• flapped	
• tulips	• flutter	
• cherry blossoms	• cluck	
• crocuses	• spectacular	

(continued on next page)

(continued from previous page)

Props/Visual Aids for Story Retelling

- Characters: paper plates, watercolor paints and/or markers to create four chickens, P. Zonka, Maud, Dora, and Nadine, and one rooster, Gloria
- One basket and four plastic eggs (white, brown, blue, and one multicolored Ukrainian decorated egg)
- Yellow and red construction paper for wattle, beak, and comb

Directions

- Create chickens by folding a paper plate in half, then decorating with either paint or markers or both.
- Add construction paper wattle, beak, and comb.
- Using props, retell the story either by enacting with a group or manipulating the props as a small group, scaffolding the retelling when needed to ensure a positive experience until children can move toward independence in retelling on their own.

Differentiation Strategies

- To simplify the experience, the teacher acts as director and narrator and cues children in their roles as chickens.
- To make the retelling more challenging, ask children to reconstruct and retell the story on their own using the props.

Additional Concepts

Barnyard, farms, cultural practices in decorating eggs (*pysanka* or Ukrainian decorated eggs)

Sparking Exploratory Play (What would happen if . . . ?)

- . . . P. Zonka's egg hatched? Would the chick look like the other chicks? How would it act? What would it do? What adventures would P. Zonka and her chick have together?

Self-Awareness: Building Self-Esteem and Appreciating Differences

Wild About Us! by Karen Beaumont and illustrated by Janet Stevens (2015)

Photographs representing animals in the book were mounted on card stock and laminated as visual aids for retelling this story.

Summary of the Story

Warthog points out several identifying characteristics of certain zoo animals and presents them in a positive way (these same characteristics could be viewed negatively). With a rhyming text and delightful, supportive illustrations, the book engages young children from start to finish.

Why This Book Has Potential for Story Retelling

Because children will be engaged and delighted with the illustrations, they will love exploring animal features further in authentic photographs of each animal depicted in the story. This concept book on animal features has an accompanying message of celebrating differences and accepting them in ourselves and each other. The text and especially the illustrations, coupled with photos of real animals, offer potential for exploring descriptive language of zoo animals.

(continued on next page)

(continued from previous page)

Vocabulary

- warthog
- crocodile
- rhino
- elephant
- giraffe
- flamingo
- potbellied pig
- tortoise
- porcupine
- leopard
- hippo
- chimp
- kangaroo
- tusks
- warts
- confident
- lanky
- plump
- behind
- jiggles
- charming
- pout
- glad
- shame
- same and different

Relationship Strategies Addressed in the Story

- Accept one's own and others' physical features by identifying and acknowledging these features and appreciating them.
- Acknowledge and promote difference over sameness.

Props/Visual Aids for Story Retelling

- Thirteen animals are in this story, and each deserves either a picture or a puppet, toy, stuffed animal, or any mixture thereof. If you are lucky enough to have the plastic zoo animals made to scale, use them for retelling in this case. Animals are a warthog, crocodile, rhino, elephant, giraffe, flamingo, potbellied pig, tortoise, porcupine, leopard, hippo, chimp, and kangaroo (with joey if possible).
- In the book, a fly appears on each animal and serves as continuity or grounding for the child while listening to the story. It is also a source for visual discrimination (in finding the fly). Thus, an extended prop could be a plastic fly.

Directions

- Locate photographs of each animal online and print two sets: one to represent the animals in the book and another to use for the last card (representing the last page in the book).
- Mount on card stock and laminate.
- Create a title card for the visual aids.
- To create the final card, use the second set of photos and cut them apart in a similar manner as the last page in the book (which depicts portions of all animals in the book).
- If you have a plastic fly in the classroom, put in the story-retelling container with these visual aids to serve as a visual place holder while retelling.
- Place a copy of the book with visual aids for support; children may use the visual aids to help them recall features of animals that make them unique, and they may refer to the illustrations in the book to self-check or prompt sequence.

Differentiation Strategies

- To simplify, use props (such as animal toys) instead of pictures.
- To simplify, punch a hole in the corner of each card and bind them with a ring or cord to provide sequence to the child.
- To simplify, ask the children which animals they wish to share, and remove all the cards except for the child-selected animals.
- To make the retelling very challenging, remove all cards but the last card, which has only portions of each animal represented (for a more symbolic phase of story retelling).

Additional Concepts

Animal attributes, descriptive words, and zoo animals

Sparking Exploratory Play (What would happen if . . . ?)

- . . . the animals added you to their differences celebration? What would they say when introducing you?
- . . . the animals added some farm animals to their differences celebration? How would they describe the farm animals' special features in descriptive yet positive ways?

Self-Awareness: Identifying Feelings

Theo's Mood by Maryann Cocca-Leffler (2013)

This story is divided into two segments: a school segment where events are described as causes for particular emotions and a home segment that follows the pattern set in the school segment. Structure the events on two color-coded strips so children can match emotions (on faces) with events (on strips). Color coding helps children with self-checking.

Summary of the Story

Over the weekend, Theo's family expanded with the arrival of his new baby sister. When asked about his mood at school by his teacher on Mood Monday, Theo didn't know how to answer (the problem of the story). After hearing from his peers about their moods, Theo realized he was feeling many moods all at once.

Why This Book Has Potential for Story Retelling

This book is particularly effective because it shares the reason behind each mood. I also appreciate the author-illustrator's method of telling the story of Theo and his moods. Cocca-Leffler first introduces six different moods with six children who explain them before repeating the pattern with Theo (who ends up feeling all six moods at once). In doing so, an element of predictability emerges with the repetition.

Vocabulary

- mood
- happy
- jealous
- afraid
- sad
- mad
- proud

Self-Awareness Strategies Addressed in the Story

- Thinking about what happened and why may help us understand our emotions.
- Listening to others talk about their feelings can help us understand our own feelings.

Props/Visual Aids for Story Retelling

- Two storyboard strips, each with six frames
- One copy of the coloring sheet created for the book on the author's website (cut apart and copied)

Directions

- On the author/illustrator's website (maryanncoccaleffler.com), pull up the coloring sheet that includes facial expressions and emotion labels for each character of the book.
- Cover Theo's mouth and the word *grateful* in the label on the author's coloring sheet with Wite-Out. Make six photocopies of this blank Theo.
- Create each of Theo's six moods depicted in the book by drawing mouths and their labels in the blank spaces.
- Sketch out two storyboard frames (one for school and one for home) by providing a simple sketch of one key component per event in the story sequence. I drew a bicycle to represent *happy* and a trophy to depict *jealous*, for example. Clip art could be used instead of sketches. By organizing the story into two linear frames representing each of the two segments (one for school, the second for home), children can match schoolchildren with events that cause emotions that were reported at school, then match Theo with emotions he felt at home. Each story frame offers a key symbol of an event leading to the mood as told in the story.
- Children retell the story by matching the character to the event on the storyboard frame—first using the school storyboard frame, then Theo's storyboard frame.
- See Recommended Resources for additional information.

(continued on next page)

(continued from previous page)

Differentiation Strategies	Additional Concepts

Differentiation Strategies

- To scaffold children toward success in early retelling, I color-coded each event with its matching facial expression by using the same color paper for each mood (so green represented a jealous face *and* the matching event that led to jealousy). Children match the face with the event while retelling, and the color coding makes the matching simpler.
- To further simplify, provide children with the first six frames of the story prematched with the facial expression. In this case, children will need to recall a shorter portion of the story by using a storyboard (much like pretend reading of a book).
- To make the story-retelling props more challenging for children, cut apart the story frames so children may match faces with events and put them in sequence for retelling.

Additional Concepts

New baby, school experiences (such as morning routine), and reflecting on past events

Sparking Exploratory Play (What would happen if . . . ?)

- . . . you picked one of the six remaining characters (from the first half of the book) and enacted their stories with more details than are in the book?

Self-Awareness: Belonging

Little Elliot: Big Family by Mike Curato (2015)

Simple felt mouse and elephant puppets were created as props for this story of friendship, family, and belonging. By folding white paper accordion style, then cutting simple mice figures with connecting arms, simple props to represent the mice family members were made.

Summary of the Story

This is part of a series of books about Mouse and Little Elliot, the pink-and-blue polka-dot elephant. Mouse goes to a family reunion, and Little Elliot feels left out and lonely until Mouse invites him to join his family and Elliot realizes he belongs even though he is not related to the group.

Why This Book Has Potential for Story Retelling

What makes this book particularly nice for story retelling is the simplicity of having two main characters who are best friends and care about each other. The plot is simple, and the story can be enacted as a small group or large group, allowing those who are not playing roles of Mouse and Elliot to participate as the mice family members in the background.

Vocabulary

- family reunion
- chowder
- grandmother
- extra large
- batch
- theater
- lonely
- blanketed in white

Relationship Strategies Addressed in the Story

- Belonging involves participation and enjoying others.
- Invite others and encourage participation by giving a warm welcome and including them in the games.

Props/Visual Aids for Story Retelling

- Create simple puppets for the characters Little Elliot, Mouse, and lots of mouse relatives.
- Supplementary props could include bottle caps for plates as used in the book, or small dollhouse furniture such as a small table or rocking chair. I cut out a string of mice (to represent the family) and put them in a circle as one prop.

Directions

- Retell or enact the story while manipulating props as a group, coconstructing the story together.

Differentiation Strategies

- To simplify, add a storyboard to support plot sequence.
- To make story retelling more challenging, have children retell without group collaboration, as individuals or pairs.

Additional Concepts

Friendships and families

Sparking Exploratory Play (What would happen if . . . ?)

- . . . Elliot, Mouse, and Mouse's family went outside to play in the snow during the family reunion?
- . . . Mouse was invited to Elliot's family reunion?

Self-Management: Controlling Emotions and Problem Solving When Emotions Get Out of Control

Bernice Gets Carried Away by Hannah E. Harrison (2015)

This photo depicts two ways to retell the story. First, by using nothing more than paper birthday hats, children can enact the plot events in the story by miming the actions. Second, a story-in-a-box includes a setting as the background when opened and a simple finger puppet for each character in the book. Bird and Squirrel, minor characters in the book, are glued to the background because they never move in the story.

Summary of the Story

Bernice is invited to her friend Bear's birthday party, but nothing goes right for her, building her frustration. Finally, when she's had enough, she takes all the balloons for herself and literally gets carried away. She realizes that sharing the balloons will help her resolve her problems and get her back to the ground.

Why This Book Has Potential for Story Retelling

Children can relate to the story and will identify with the birthday party setting and events. The plot is simple and includes a problem easily resolved. The richness of the story combined with the simplicity of the narrative structure make it a find for enacting or retelling with different group sizes and developmental levels.

Vocabulary

- horrible
- dreary
- mood
- prune
- grapefruit
- piñata
- smithereens
- bad mood
- surly
- blue (as in the mood)
- brooding
- peered

Relationship Strategies Addressed in the Story

- Things don't always go our way, and we need to control or manage our emotions when that happens.
- Sharing is one way to make a responsible decision.

Props/Visual Aids for Story Retelling

- Make or find finger puppets or other props to represent each of the characters: Cat (Bernice), Pig, Turtle, Bear, Fox, Rabbit, and White Goose.
- Create (to scale of finger puppets or props) fake balloons, and if desired, a squirrel and a bluebird.
- Create a reversible felt (happy/sad face) cloud for the sky in the setting.
- A second option is to provide seven birthday party hats for children to wear as costumes for an enactment.

Directions

- Create a story-in-a-box with the setting included on a large "wall" of the box. A tree is a prominent part of the setting and houses the squirrel and the bird on branches.
- In my example, only the cloud can be changed (to happy or sad by reversing it) in the background setting—which keeps the focus of the story on the characters.
- If the sky is made of felt, a felt cloud will stick without Velcro. Retell or enact using props.
- To extend the characters to involve more children in the retelling, make bird and squirrel finger puppets. If made of felt, they will stay on the felt background.

(continued on next page)

(continued from previous page)

Differentiation Strategies	Additional Concepts

Differentiation Strategies

- To simplify, enact the story as an orchestrated play with the teacher as director and narrator, prompting children with roles and actions—in fact, the story encourages group retellings in this manner because there is much narration and few character lines.
- To make the retelling more challenging, move toward "compatible pair" retellings, independent retellings, or fewer props.

Additional Concepts

Birthday party, animals who live in trees, and weather

Sparking Exploratory Play (What would happen if . . . ?)

- . . . Bernice chose not to share and kept all the balloons?
- . . . Bernice had her own party and invited everyone to come? What would be different about Bernice's party?

Self-Management: Persistence

The Red Hat by David Teague, illustrated by Antoinette Portis (2015)

Simple props are put together by using blocks, wooden people, red construction paper, black embroidery floss, and red felt.

Summary of the Story

A little boy with a red scarf lives on top of a building where he observes a new building under construction. A little girl with a red hat moves into the new building and, like the boy, goes to the top of her building to observe the world. The boy makes multiple attempts to meet the girl from atop the building but is foiled by the wind every time (which also blows away the girl's red hat). He persists and finally meets her by returning her red hat, which he found as he walked to visit her in person (rather than be foiled by the wind once again).

Why This Book Has Potential for Story Retelling

The story includes multiple small problems that build to a crescendo, much like more sophisticated narratives, yet the book remains simple and predictable. It can be enacted or retold by one or two children together, or more children can take turns to enact segments of the story.

(continued on next page)

(continued from previous page)

Vocabulary

- tallest
- whisked
- snatched
- glided
- spun
- kite and tail
- earflaps
- dropped
- yanked
- corners
- captured
- roared
- swooped
- swirled
- soared
- reached
- swept
- stole
- down
- raged
- bellowed
- boulevards
- howled and yowled
- alleyways

Relationship Strategies Addressed in the Story

Persistence with a bit of trial and error paves the way to success.

Props/Visual Aids for Story Retelling

- Two people (I chose wooden people with no facial expressions to enact this story).
- Create a red scarf for the boy and a red hat for the girl (I used red felt).
- Use blocks for building two towers.
- Additional props: pencil (for writing a note), red paper (for folding into an airplane), red kite with white tail (such as a narrow strip of paper), and a small red blanket prop made out of felt.

Directions

- Begin by having children build a tower with blocks. Put Billy Hightower, complete with his red scarf, on the top.
- Build a second tower, adding the little girl with the red hat.
- Continue enacting while retelling the story with the remaining props.
- Consider keeping the block towers intact for the duration of the story-retelling focus (a corner spot protected by orange cones might help keep the towers intact for a week or so).
- In the later retelling sessions with completed towers, engage with the small group by coconstructing the story together as a review process with the existing block towers, followed by enacting the story with teacher narration and prompts as heavy support, gradually allowing children more independence in their retellings and enactments during small-group time.
- Alternately, enact the story with children wearing a dress-up red hat and red scarf playing the roles. They can pretend to use an authentic kite, paper airplane, and red blanket, respectively, and pretend to be on top of tall buildings.

Differentiation Strategies

- To simplify, give children a storyboard structure from which to reference during retelling—consider taking photographs of the props at various plot events as part of the storyboard to support the enactment or retelling with props.
- To provide more complexity, offer only a few visual aids of key plot events; photos of the props at key plot events will serve nicely.

Additional Concepts

Making friends, properties of the wind, city skyscrapers

Sparking Exploratory Play (What would happen if . . . ?)

- . . . the story took place on a farm? At the zoo? On a beach?
- . . . the story continued? (At the end of the story, Billy and the girl are friends, and instead of ending with the typical "the end," the story ends with "the beginning." So what's next?)

Social Awareness: Consequences of Not Helping/Incentive to Help and Cooperate

The Little Red Hen by Jerry Pinkney (2006)

Pulling one goat puppet from *The Three Billy Goats Gruff* set and one pig puppet from *The Three Little Pigs* completed the set of puppets needed to retell *The Little Red Hen*.

Summary of the Story

Little Red Hen finds some seeds and, with the help of her friends, learns that if she plants them, the seeds will grow into wheat that can be ground to make bread. The author takes us through the process of planting, harvesting, threshing, milling or grinding, and baking in the story—all conducted by a little red hen who gets no help from her friends. As a result, the friends do not get to eat the bread at the end of the story. This classic tale, gorgeously illustrated, gives young children complex vocabulary-building experiences with authentic learning.

Why This Book Has Potential for Story Retelling

The potential for familiarity to the child (as a classic tale) plus the repetitive text make this a wonderful story for young children to retell. The consequences suffered at the end for those who did not help bake the bread make this story highly motivating.

Vocabulary

- hen
- cheery
- scooped
- wheat
- "scratched for food"
- planting
- harvest
- thresh
- separate
- ground (grind)
- bake
- grain
- mill
- jam

Relationship Strategies Addressed in the Story

- If we don't help or contribute, our friend has no reason to share with us.
- If we help or contribute, our friend may share or contribute back.

Props/Visual Aids for Story Retelling

- Find or make costumes or any type of prop for these characters: Little red hen, short brown dog, thin gray rat, tall black goat, and round pink pig. Secondary characters could include the miller and five yellow chicks.
- Additional props to enhance the retelling: Wheat, jar of jam, pretend (or real) bread loaf from the kitchen center.

Directions

- Retell with props, costumes drawn from the book, puppets, or toys.
- Because there are repeating phrases—"Who will help me?" by the Little Red Hen and "Not I" by four of the characters—the story lends itself to enactments in preschool, often with the teacher as director/narrator and the children as the main characters, saying the short, repeating lines.
- As children grow in their understanding, vocabulary, and retelling skills, they may take on responsibility for more of the story narrative.

(continued on next page)

(continued from previous page)

Differentiation Strategies	Additional Concepts
• To simplify the retelling for enacting as a class or large group, the teacher serves as narrator and director with children supplying their lines only. • For individual retelling with the novice reteller, begin with the main characters only and expect fewer details, then grow the story details with additional props, scaffolding along the way. • To make the story retelling more challenging, provide visual aids of key plot events and characters to retell the story.	Growing wheat, harvesting, threshing, milling, and baking bread **Sparking Exploratory Play (What would happen if … ?)** • … the friends say, "Yes, I'll help you!" • … the Little Red Hen opened a bakery to sell her bread to others?

Social Awareness: Kindness

If You Plant a Seed by Kadir Nelson (2015)

Essential to retelling this story are the rabbit and mouse, but the book has nearly unlimited potential for nature and gardening props—it is just a matter of gathering.

Summary of the Story	Why This Book Has Potential for Story Retelling
This book explores the consequences played out in two different scenarios when a rabbit and mouse plant and tend a carrot, cabbage, and tomato seed: being selfish (not sharing) or being kind or caring (sharing with others). As one would expect, chaos and unhappiness ensue in the selfish scenario, while a bountiful harvest increases when sharing and kindness are practiced.	Bigger-than-life, colorful illustrations with minimum text make this a highly engaging story for children. A few pages of wordless pictures provide opportunities for teacher-child coconstruction of text. The plot structure plays out both selfishness and sharing scenarios, which also engage children. It's a great story for social-emotional curriculum because the consequences of both scenarios are played out and potential for meaningful dialogue results.

Vocabulary	Relationship Strategies Addressed in the Story
• tomato • selfishness • carrot • heap • cabbage • trouble • seeds • kindness • plants	• The alternative strategy of kindness over selfishness bringing friendships, cooperation, and rewards comes clear through illustrations and text.

(continued on next page)

(continued from previous page)

Props/Visual Aids for Story Retelling

- Mouse finger puppet and bunny hand puppet (or toys) are crucial to the retelling.
- The various birds as supporting cast could easily be played with stuffed animals (the true-to-life plush birds from the science center that make authentic birdcalls are enticing).
- A garden setting, complete with seeds, plants, and fake sunflowers in the end will make this story perfect for story acting with a small group or whole class.

Directions

- Retell the story with puppets, stuffed birds, and various props depicting the setting and characters.

Differentiation Strategies

- To simplify, provide more scaffolding and start with just the key characters, adding props and directing children.
- To challenge the story reteller to be more independent, withdraw scaffolding as he or she retells the story.
- For a more challenging retelling, allow the child to be in charge of props and the story, prompting only when help is requested.

Additional Concepts

Gardening, animals' nutritional needs, and how real animals are similar to and different from this story

Sparking Exploratory Play (What would happen if . . . ?)

- . . . new friends created a grocery store with their harvest?

Relationship Skills: Asking Someone to Be a Friend

Do You Want to Be My Friend? by Eric Carle (1976)

Two ways to retell this story are depicted: visual aids and props. Two old copies of Carle's book are cut apart and pieced together to create visual aids. Similarly, the basket includes props for retelling composed of a plush long snake and miscellaneous toys representative of animals in the book.

Summary of the Story

In this mostly wordless picture book, a little mouse asks each animal he passes, "Do you want to be my friend?" until finally, the little mouse meets a friend. The presence of a snake at the bottom of the page offers both continuity and grounding for the story as well as a bit of a threat or drama.

Why This Book Has Potential for Story Retelling

This book is a classic for a reason: children and families love it! Carle capitalizes on the page turn for building wonder and curiosity by placing the tail of the upcoming animal on one page, inevitably creating a guessing game for what is to come. The constant threat of the snake builds tension for young children near the end of the story. The wordless nature of the book encourages story retelling while "reading."

(continued on next page)

(continued from previous page)

Vocabulary

The book is a nearly wordless picture book, but facing the title page are suggestions for wording.

- outdoors
- friend
- elephant
- mice
- snake
- horse
- crocodile
- lion
- hippo
- seal
- monkey
- peacock
- fox
- kangaroo
- giraffe
- hole
- tree trunk
- tree roots

Relationship Strategies Addressed in the Story

- Keep asking (persist) others to find a friend.
- Respect a "no" answer, or a "not right now," or a lack of a response from an individual . . . by moving on and checking with others.

Props/Visual Aids for Story Retelling

- To make visual aids, I used two old copies of the paperback book for cutting out the animals, backing them with card stock, and laminating them.
- Create the long snake by cutting it out of the two books, backing the strips with card stock, and laminating.
- You may either ask children to lay the animal pictures on top of the snake or add a Velcro piece to the snake and backing to the animal to attach in sequence and make up one's own words in the story-retelling experience.
- To bring the story to life, consider adding two finger-puppet mice.
- An alternative is to use props such as plush animals or toys (note: on the cover, the mouse asks an elephant for his friendship; although not in the story, the elephant could be added because it is part of the cover and appears to start the story before its real beginning).
- See Recommended Resources for additional information.

Directions

- In this nearly wordless picture book, it is important to model the language for children while reading. The author offers an example in his note to teachers and parents.
- For interactive group retellings, distribute the animals and mice to children (with the exception of the snake, which should remain up front with the teacher or facilitator). Telling the story as a class, children can each attach one animal to the snake as the mouse asks, "Do you want to be my friend?"
- For centers: Children enjoy retelling the story with props in the library center (alone and in pairs or small groups). The length of the snake is joyful for children for retelling. Plan for its path in advance when children retell in centers: consider a hallway or along the perimeter or center of the classroom, modeling and outlining the retelling path to children in advance during whole-group meetings so the entire class is aware of special space needs for this center while these props are in the room.

(continued on next page)

(continued from previous page)

Differentiation Strategies

- Story retelling with props (toys or models) is considered simpler than using visual aids (pictures). The most simplistic way to retell this story is to do it as a group with heavy teacher support as narrator and director.
- To support simplifying small-group or individual retellings, keep a copy of the book close by and also consider adding a storyboard to prompt the next animal in the sequence.
- To make the story more complex, use the visual aids with no storyboard prompt nearby.

Additional Concepts

Animal names, mice live underground, and snakes eat mice

Sparking Exploratory Play (What would happen if . . . ?)

- . . . one or more animals played with the first mouse during the story?
- . . . there was no hole for the mice to hide at the end? Where would they go? What would they do? Could the mice talk to the other animals? What would they say?

Relationship Skills: Taking Perspectives

A Big Guy Took My Ball! by Mo Willems (2013)

Interestingly, when I tested props with preschool children, they chose elephant and pig finger-puppet props over the commercial plush replica of Elephant and Piggy. Finger puppets hold great appeal to young children. The whale is a handpuppet. For lack of a yellow Ping-Pong ball, I created one out of card stock.

Summary of the Story

Piggy asks Gerald (the elephant) to help him get his ball back from a very large animal who took it. Elephant tries to help, but a turn of events causes them to take a different perspective. Young children may see two problems in this book: Piggy loses his ball (small problem) and Gerald the elephant fails to get it back for him. Gerald and Piggy learn that the ball is not really Piggy's ball but instead belongs to Whale. How will Gerald and Piggy get to play with the ball? How can Whale get a friend?

Why This Book Has Potential for Story Retelling

The simple props appeal to young children, and lack of setting make most Gerald and Piggy stories prime for retelling or enacting. Most Elephant and Piggy books have social-emotional themes. This one is a terrific choice.

(continued on next page)

(continued from previous page)

Vocabulary

- upset
- big
- bigger
- small
- smaller
- excuse me
- thank you

Relationship Strategies Addressed in the Story

- Listen to the other person's story to understand what's happening.
- Inviting a person to play with you can sometimes solve a problem, especially if the person is sad or lonely or has a ball.

Props/Visual Aids for Story Retelling

- Retelling this book requires three character props—whether they are puppets, pictures, costumes, or something else—and a small ball.
- If using toys, it is important to keep scale in mind when selecting props because of the author's use of vocabulary relating to size: blue whale (the largest of them all), gray elephant (much smaller than the whale; the elephant wears glasses, though my elephant finger puppet does not); pink pig (smaller than the elephant); and the yellow ball (smallest of all) with lovely red spots.

Directions

- Retell or enact with props.

Differentiation Strategies

- To simplify the retelling, add a story structure path with photo bubbles as support. The first photo bubble holds a picture of Piggy complaining to Gerald, the second of Gerald approaching the whale, the third of the whale explaining his friendless situation to Gerald and Piggy, and the last with all three playing with the ball together. This is a typical fictional story map in children's literature, with smaller problems leading to larger ones before the resolution happens either near or at the end.
- To challenge students, provide fewer props and less teacher support or move toward key visual aids.

Additional Concepts

Bullying (in this case, taking things that are not yours), sharing, friendships, loneliness, sadness, getting upset, worrying, good manners, and size relationships (big, bigger, small)

Sparking Exploratory Play (What would happen if . . . ?)

- . . . we created a setting? Where would this story take place?

Responsible Decision Making

All for Me and None for All by Helen Lester, illustrated by Lynn Munsinger (2012)

Hand puppets are made from colored paper or plastic cups to represent characters in this book and are something children can make as well.

Summary of the Story

This story is about the consequences for a greedy pig named Gruntly who takes everything for himself—very irresponsible decision making for building social relationships. As a result, his friends grow tired of his greediness. One day he participates in a treasure hunt and is the last one to arrive on the scene. His kind friends saved his portion for him, and he is so moved by their generosity, he makes a responsible decision: he shares.

Why This Book Has Potential for Story Retelling

The book is a wonderful pick because it enables children to safely explore selfishness and greed (and their consequences) in a rather exaggerated way through Gruntly's character. I love that the character changes at the end of the story by coming to an awareness of others. The story itself depicts self-to-otherness in a very relatable (to children) way.

Vocabulary

- hog
- fluff
- poofiest
- companions
- fed-up
- greediness
- wolfing
- illegal
- treasure
- park ranger
- stupendously superb opportunity
- hissed
- number one
- clue
- racing
- sea
- snorted
- "scusi"
- tipped
- stressful
- strutted
- snatched
- grabbed
- nibble
- gobble
- hogged
- trembling
- worried

Relationship Strategies Addressed in the Story

- We learn the strategy of being kind to others.
- Modeling kindness, fairness, and generosity to others, even though they may not be fair with us, can help others learn to be fair or generous.

(continued on next page)

(continued from previous page)

Props/Visual Aids for Story Retelling

- Characters: three pigs, a dog, a chicken, and a sheep.
- Extra props might include a pair of doll or baby shoes, a doll pillow, fake daisies, a donut from the house center, three paper "clues" numbered as Clue #1, #2, and #3, and six small pretend sacks for some pretend trail mix.

Directions

- Retell or enact using the main characters and add props as desired to provoke children's memories of the details and sequence of the story. This story is more sophisticated and less familiar to children (compared to *The Three Little Pigs*, for example), so scaffolding is likely needed either as an enactment with teacher narration or direction or in story retelling with props.

Differentiation Strategies

- To simplify the retelling or enactment, re-create settings from the book on poster board and mount on the wall (or rest on a chalk tray) at the child's level for moving from one key plot event to another in book sequence. Settings may be created simply by sketching key features of a particular scene, such as a swing set or log on each poster. Characters may visit each setting by moving from left to right, which will serve as a prompt for what comes next in the story.
- To make the retelling more complex, have children retell with less support.

Additional Concepts

Friends and sharing

Sparking Exploratory Play (What would happen if . . . ?)

- . . . if the animals played a ball game afterward? Would Gruntly share the balls with others, or would he hoard the balls?

Supporting Children's STEM Inquiries through Story Retelling

Story retelling has a place in STEM inquiries, projects, and themes when we use books to kick off a study about honeybees or wheels or the wind. The child pictured at the beginning of this chapter is in the midst of exploring plant roots. Although she's had experiences with flowers and flowering plants, the roots have been off limits—exploring roots is a new experience for her. She is using a magnifying glass to get a closer look. She knows to be gentle in her explorations so the plant can live. Later she will document her plant through an observational drawing, striving for accuracy. When teachers structure learning to include data collection, children are able to use mathematics to quantify, describe, and notice patterns. The flowers are circle shaped. We can count the stems and the leaves on one stem. We might wonder why watering a plant makes the plant heavy to carry and why it gets lighter in weight when it needs more water. Where does the water go?

"It looks like spaghetti!"

Purchasing plants at a garden center and then planting them at school offers children opportunities to enact story retelling in very authentic and connected ways, especially when they study about plants, flowers, or gardening at the same time.

Beginning a study of flowers with Eve Bunting's *Flower Garden* eases children into the fascinating and gorgeous world of flowers through pictures and a relatable story (2000). The story is of an African American child who, with the help of her father, purchases garden flowers and takes them home on the bus to plant in a window box as a gift for her mother's birthday. This is a rich story for young children and teachers alike because it lets us retell and revisit concepts again and again through several meaningful ways.

First, the story lends itself to actually visiting a garden center to purchase flowers for a window box. Planting flowers in a window box for the science center will require potting soil, garden tools, newspaper, and a watering can. STEM inquiries engage children in authentic, real phenomena of study. Second, the book serves for story retelling and enacting experiences with props such as plastic flowers, pots, and window boxes. Third, free-play experiences with these same props should produce interesting variations on the original story and hold potential to foster explorations of story-related vocabulary. When coupled with an authentic STEM project on plants, the richness in vocabulary and conceptual development becomes exponential.

Additional story retelling also has a place in the middle of STEM work as we learn scientific information about our topic of study from a resource or nonfiction book, such as Aloian's *What Are Bulbs and Roots?* (2012). After finding out key information, we communicate with others through retelling a portion of the story of roots. Story retelling may also serve at the end of a project when we share our information in a play about seeds growing into plants. Each child might take on a role, such as that of a seed or plant, or one of several narrators to explain the function of each particular part of the plant. We are retelling key, applicable information found in nonfiction books, likely basic concepts attached to rich vocabulary.

Early childhood teachers have been integrating domains of learning for years, so the concept of teaching holistically is nothing new. What is relatively new is intentionality in integrating the STEM disciplines of science, technology, engineering, and mathematics for young children. Whereas yesterday's early childhood teachers may have ended the study of gardens with putting plastic flowers and pots in the house center for free play, planting flowers, or creating art related to flowers and gardens, today's early childhood teacher will integrate science tools to conduct a science exploration of roots firsthand and identify other parts of the plant. Teachers and children will ask questions and make observations, find out information, and collect data by using mathematics to measure, count, or identify shapes and patterns. Children create an observational drawing of a plant and, if they wish to do so, label the parts of a plant. Today's teacher might use an iPad to share a YouTube video on how plants take minerals and water from soil. Whereas yesterday's early childhood teacher capitalized on incidental science, today's educator considers how to merge at least two STEM areas together with intentionality to facilitate conceptual depth, process skills, and critical thinking.

Key to STEM projects, themes, and inquiries is actually doing science: the presence of science objects to manipulate (like pulleys or tubes or chimes) or phenomena (the item of study or a real object). Real science requires real stuff. Having something real is necessary for bringing the text found in science books to life.

Pictures that accompany the words in *From Seed to Plant,* a beloved and long-lasting nonfiction book about plants created with young learners in mind, are simply compelling (Gibbons 1991). They offer a cross-section of the soil and plant to demonstrate the fascinating work of roots. A nonfiction read-aloud, however, may not capture young children's interests as well as a good story. When children have experiences in exploring, growing, and observing real plants—flowers, stems, leaves, and roots planted in soil—they have potential to develop deep conceptual understanding when their explorations are accompanied by a great book. Children can pose a question and, with teacher support, find out information, investigate a hypothesis, and apply critical thinking. They might revisit this study later in the year by growing a plant from a seed, observing plants in nature, planting bulbs in school yards, or discovering that pods, pinecones, and acorns are really seeds. Revisiting inquiry projects builds conceptual depth. An exploration into STEM concepts and expectations for young children's learning certainly can be motivated by the STEM topic alone. Science is fascinating! Selecting stories for retelling that support and even motivate STEM activities gives children a common experience together—a place to kick off a meaningful study.

This labeled drawing was created with the encouragement of the teacher. At first the child asked to have the teacher help with accurate spelling. After helping with two words, the teacher encouraged the child to write on her own and helped her sound out the words. Doing so allowed the teacher to gauge developmental progression in writing.

The NSTA Early Childhood Science Education Position Statement

The NSTA position statement on science education was endorsed by NAEYC in 2014 and serves to guide our work with young children in science education. The NSTA Early Childhood Science Education position statement honors the development of the young child by first holding that young children (ages three to five) use observation, exploration, and discovery as "basic abilities for science learning" (10). These key skills are fundamental to early childhood science education.

In addition to highlighting basic abilities for early childhood science education, NSTA recognizes that young children are quite capable of learning and understanding science concepts. Further, NSTA advocates that young children can "use the practices of reasoning and inquiry" (2014, 11). Acknowledging that young children need curriculum that allows for "deep exploration of important concepts" (NRC 2012, 25), the NSTA Position Statement indicates that young children can be engaged in science over long periods of time instead of a single session or activity. NSTA offers the following key principles for guiding science learning in young children.

- "Children have the capacity to engage in scientific practices and develop understanding at a conceptual level."
- "Adults play a central and important role in helping young children learn science."
- "Young children need multiple and varied opportunities to engage in science exploration and discovery."
- "Young children develop science skills and knowledge in both formal and informal settings."
- "Young children develop science skills and knowledge over time."
- "Young children develop science skills and learning by engaging in experiential learning." (10–11)

Developing "Practices" of Inquiry and Reasoning

Nurturing inquiry involves teaching to facilitate language development and meaning in the context of authentic experiences. Science and engineering "practices" validate that children use both knowledge and skills while engaged in inquiry (NRC 2012, 42). When teachers ask children questions in science and pose problems in engineering, they draw out children's thinking, language, and current knowledge. When children pose a problem or ask a question, they are developing skills and tools for seeking solutions or information. Questions are at the heart of inquiry and are considered a key practice for learning and investigating. We're mining for intellectual gold when we ask questions of children. Similarly, teachers may model how to find out information by observation, through investigation, or by looking for information online.

Additional practices such as drawing, sketching, and making models help children notice details and develop visual-spatial skills as well as eye-hand coordination. Making predictions and guesses help children build foundations for more sophisticated hypotheses later. Investigating questions or testing solutions facilitates children's social-emotional needs for putting their plans in action. Collecting data when observing builds mathematics skills: counting, identifying shapes, telling about changes or causes and relationships, or noticing patterns, for example. The practice of sharing results and communicating learning with others is supported by nonfiction story retelling.

To illustrate science and engineering practices further, consider this inquiry into bees. The teacher began the study by sharing a honeycomb she found at a farmers market. Children employed the practice of observation when they viewed honeycombs with magnifying glasses, using their sense of sight to notice details and patterns. From the observation experience, children applied the practice of asking questions, which the teacher wrote down and posted in the science center, where the honeycomb stayed in its container. Another day, children used the practice of predicting, when they guessed how many cells (the hexagons created by the bees) were in the honeycomb. They applied the practice of data collection when they counted the visible cells in the honeycomb (mathematics connection). Another day, they completed their practice of observational drawings. The teacher documented children's key observation(s) underneath the drawing. One child asked a question about how it would feel to touch the honeycomb while another asked about how it might taste. The practice of creating hypotheses about these questions provided rich dialogue and the sharing of personal experiences with honey.

A study of honeybees offers children opportunities to develop science practices. Nonfiction story retelling serves as a structure for communicating information with others, integral to the "practice" of communicating findings with others.

On another day, children carried out the practice of investigation by cutting the honeycomb with a plastic knife and making observations based on sense of sight, touch, and taste. Anticipating a potential sticky situation in small-group time, the teacher prepared children ahead of time and had wipes close at hand. They tasted honey on bread, and those who wished to do so chewed a small sample of the wax—the teacher prepared them by equating wax to chewing gum, noting it shouldn't be swallowed and discussing what they could do with the wax once it was chewed. More questions ensued about how honey and honeycombs are made. The teacher found a short video on beehives and bee communication strategies (the bee dance) online to share with her young students.

Story retelling fits into the inquiry project in two ways: (1) when children shared information learned from nonfiction texts, a science and engineering practice of communicating ideas, both during and at the end of the project, and (2) when they participated in an ongoing fictional story-retelling project throughout the study of the honeycomb using Eric Carle's related book *The Honeybee and the Robber* (2001). In summary, posing questions of phenomena, predicting quantity, testing hypotheses through investigation, answering questions, explaining, making drawings and observations, and sharing new knowledge are science practices experienced by children authentically. This project included connections mainly to the life sciences and mathematics, though one could make a case that the use of magnifying glasses and the bee-dance video engaged children with technology.

STEM Content Learning in Early Childhood Education

Current thinking in STEM content for young children offers early childhood teachers a wide range of topics from which to choose. Typically, for preschool children, meaningful studies focus on engaging children with language-rich science experiences. Making observations of clouds or the surprising moon that sometimes appears in the morning or the insects that cross our paths as we walk and play outdoors is interesting to children because clouds, the moon, and insects are an important part of their world. We explore sand and rocks and pebbles outside and bring them inside to the sensory table for further explorations. We make "geology shakes" and learn about sedimentation (Moomaw 2013, 92) with those same rocks, pebbles, and sand when added to water in containers. We observe the sun and rainbows and investigate light diffusion when we put a flashlight in front of a prism. Because balls are important to us in a study of motion, we test the paths of marbles by dropping them in paint and watching them roll around in a box. By moving beyond the interactive read-aloud and story retelling toward coupling meaningful and relevant STEM experiences with interactions and science practices, we are forming deeper concepts and foundations for K–12 STEM education.

This child is engaged in tracking the movement of a marble dipped in paint. Questions from the teacher keep students highly engaged with interaction related to inquiry, prediction, and testing predictions. "What happens to the marble if you tip the box to the other corner?" "Where do you think it will go?" "Did the marble travel in the path you thought it would travel?"

Science

Physical science is the study of physics and chemistry (NRC 2012, 102). In the physical sciences, we learn an overarching concept: cause and effect. Physical science concepts applicable to early childhood are matter and its interactions, motion and stability, and forces and interaction. In early childhood education, this relates to our work with children in ramps and pathways or inclines (DeVries and Sales 2011). Physics inquiries include cooking activities while using tools such as sifters, colanders, sieves, and juicers. We are studying physics when we explore properties of bubbles, light and color, and pulleys or pendulums. Moomaw demystifies the use of ropes, pulleys, pendulums, and magnets with young children and offers meaningful, authentic activities for classroom studies (2013). The National Research Council offers that in the physical sciences, we are learning two core ideas: "What is everything made of?" and "Why do things happen?", certainly questions children ask naturally (2012,104).

Life science focuses on all living things: their "patterns, processes, and relationships" (NRC 2012, 139). For young children, we utilize what is relevant to them and their experiences at school, outdoors, and in the community—again, focusing on what is observable and authentic to children's interests. In learning about life sciences in early childhood, we gather an understanding that plants and animals have certain needs and explore their attributes as well as their growth cycles. Children notice the changes in themselves as they have grown from babies to young children. They notice changes in plants and animals in the world around us. Children learn how to take care of and appreciate living things in their surroundings. They learn to identify living things and separate them from nonliving things.

Earth and space science has geology as its cornerstone (NRC 2012). It technically includes the study of the biosphere, geosphere, atmosphere, and hydrosphere—weather, seasons, rocks, shells, soil, sand, pebbles, shadows, and water are part of earth and space science. Young children can observe the sky: its rainbows, its sun, its moon, and the stars. We can learn about where water is found on our earth and that water changes form to become a solid called ice or snow under certain conditions. We learn that water also changes form again under different conditions to make clouds. Water comes back to us as rain under other conditions.

Technology

Using technology for teaching and learning is becoming more commonplace in early childhood classrooms. Technology serves several roles: a tool for learning or finding out information, a topic of study, and a way to document learning.

We might use technology in STEM education when we use items such as measuring tapes, scales, timers, measuring spoons, magnifying glasses, or thermometers, for example, to help us explore or examine or experiment with materials. Although we are more used to thinking of technology as something computerized, technology also includes the use of simple tools including photography and videos. For example, we take photographs of children's work or our class project in growing bean seeds into plants at various stages of development, then print and laminate the photos to serve as a learning tool. Neumann-Hinds's book *Picture Science* serves as an inspiring resource for harnessing technology (in the form of digital photography) to nurture young children's science learning (2007). When children are provided photographs of their own work or of phenomena in their own classrooms, the photos are authentic, meaningful, and interesting. We also may use technology to look up information as we did with encyclopedias in the past.

Technology serves as a topic of study for young children when they explore simple machines. The classic simple machines typically impact force, and thus this is where technology (the machines) and physics (exploring force) intersect. Simple machines are wedges and inclines used in children's ramps and pathways work. Wedges and inclines, along with pulleys, screws, and levers, are considered simple machines, as are wheels and axles.

We use technology as a tool for documenting in many ways, such as creating audiotapes or videos of children's story-retelling episodes. We similarly photograph and collect quotes from children that reveal their thinking or make their observations visible to others. Videos and photos serve as documentation of children's learning for assessment.

Engineering

Engineering involves "designing objects, processes, and systems to meet human needs and wants," (NRC 2012, 202). Because design is core to engineering, we typically encourage children to create simple designs, then carry out their plans, which aligns with plan-do-review approaches used in High Scope. Children participate in engineering processes when they make a design (a simple drawing) followed by creating that design afterward, whether it is with blocks or tubes or pulleys or funnels and cups at the sensory table. Block structures and building with different types of materials offer children opportunities to explore different mediums for building, just as engineers choose different building materials. When we build something and a problem arises in our design, we need to solve it by understanding the problem thoroughly, then consider a change or solution in the design, try it out, and problem solve again if needed. This is the work of engineers, and teachers are in the position to identify parallels in children's work and engineering when they arise. Typically, engineering is embedded in STEM projects. Engineering is integrated in early childhood building experiences, but teachers need to serve as a bridge between the experience and the child to help children become aware of the science embedded in the activity, understand what they are experiencing, and relate their work with the work of engineers. Going back to the drawing board to design and problem solve are opportunities for "engineering" rather than signs of failure or causes of frustration.

Mathematics

Math in early childhood is often used to quantify or describe phenomena. Math is integral to data collection or describing results. For young children in preschool, curricular focal points (NCTM 2009) were identified as areas of emphasis in teaching mathematics. These focal points for preschool children center on number and operations, geometry, and measurement. Certainly STEM education engages children in applying these concepts.

Using number and operations involves several key concepts: one-to-one correspondence, cardinality (the last one in the set that was counted is the total or number); quantifying amounts; counting; comparing objects (as more, less, or equal); understanding sets (adding on or taking away or dividing the sets); and ordering sets (first, second, etc.).

Geometry involves understanding two- and three-dimensional shapes and their attributes through experiential learning. STEM projects provide children with opportunities to apply geometric vocabulary in authentic contexts, realizing that developmentally, children may identify objects early in their learning as can-shaped or ball-shaped rather than cylindrical or spherical. Geometry also includes understanding positional words in space and spatial relationships.

Building with blocks takes on new challenges when children retell together the story *Jack the Builder* by Stuart Murphy (2006). Children create structures similar to those pictured in the book, addressing spatial skills in mathematics.

In addition, children can make compositions and decompositions in space by creating pictures with pattern blocks or using blocks and knowledge of spatial relations to create composite shapes (such as arches or enclosures).

Measurement is often used in STEM projects, and in order for children to measure, they must understand what can be measured and how. Young children may measure using nonstandard and standard units of measurement in preschool and kindergarten. Measurement involves numbers regardless of whether units are standard or nonstandard. Children learn that numbers used in measurement denote size or weight. They can compare items that are measured, and they can put them in order according to size or weight.

STEM goes beyond typical math teaching emphasis areas and also engages children in using related areas of learning in math education in preschool: algebra and data analysis and probability. Algebra includes solving problems and noticing patterns and relationships. When children have access to manipulatives or other concrete objects, they can act out a problem with the manipulatives. They can solve problems with teacher support at first, then learn to be independent problem solvers themselves. Solving problems is integral to STEM experiences. Noticing patterns and relationships is part of observation. Children might notice patterns in insects or sounds or architecture, for example.

Using the skill of data analysis requires children to participate in gathering and organizing information. When teachers provide structures for creating real graphs (such as lining up the boys and lining up the girls to see how many of each are in the classroom, using one-to-one correspondence), children are able to enact the graph and understand the counting of each set. They are invested in analyzing which set is larger or if they are actually the same. Progressing young children through graphing with experiencing real graphs, then moving toward picture (iconic) graphs, and finally symbolic graphing (where we might color a square on a bar graph yellow for a sunny day) helps children understand (through experience) the concept of graphing.

Threads of Story Retelling in Early Childhood STEM Education

STEM experiences are powerful learning experiences for children. Reading and interaction over literature with children increase vocabulary. Similarly, teachers strive to help make stories come alive to children. When teachers read to children and interact over real earthworms, for example, a unique and more sophisticated vocabulary is introduced to the child: soil, aeration, and earthworms, and it's important to the child (because we have real earthworms in our classroom). Teachers who help children associate new learning with an old idea held by the child—for example, the new word *soil* to the old known word *dirt*—affect children's vocabulary learning (Gonzalez et al. 2014). STEM explorations and projects integrated with book experiences provide children with opportunities to expand their knowledge and delve more deeply into concepts beyond what is possible with a book or story retelling alone.

Finding an earthworm outdoors offers an authentic way to bring the outdoors inside, at least temporarily. Earthworms are fairly easy to keep in the classroom and are low maintenance pets.

As I mentioned earlier, story retelling plays important roles in the STEM process: (1) it supports information gathering and sharing with nonfiction literature (communicating ideas); and (2) it satisfies young children's natural penchant for play and learning with story retelling using fictional texts. Fictional story retelling enables earthworms to enter free play as props to a story (but only as plastic worms—the real ones stay in the science center) such as *Diary of a Worm* (Cronin 2003). As classroom teachers, we actually expect some of the more scientific vocabulary to enter into the play experience with the pretend worm. This is also a time for exploring how worms fit into our worlds and a place for stretching the boundaries (having worms as guests for dinner in the house center, for example). Having story-retelling centers focused on a fictional text related to the STEM study supports literacy endeavors, vocabulary, and understanding in a connected way. A caution to this approach is that historically, early childhood teachers began and ended with the pretend side of science, leaving STEM out of the picture completely.

Very young children in preschool may not know the difference between what is real and what is not real. Once, when I gave a three-year-old a pair of pretend butterfly wings, her response to me was (with the most incredible look of wonderment I've ever seen) "Will these wings make me fly?" Is it any wonder that magic feels real to a young child, considering the magical things that happen when one observes the first snowfall of the season or the almost-instant greening of the brownish-gray earth in the spring? Teachers supplement nonfiction with fictional readings related to the inquiry study. Using both types of texts allows teachers to compare texts, to focus on differences between what is real (nonfiction) and what is imagined (fiction). Teachers seize analysis opportunities by asking for instances of accuracy learned in their studies of nonfiction and applying knowledge to fictional depictions in both text and illustrations.

Nonfiction literature is used as reference material to advance our knowledge of topics of study. When we want to know something, we typically look it up. I check the index, immediately go to the correct page, find the information on the page, and read what I need to know before putting the book away and moving on. Modeling finding out information and reading just a portion of a nonfiction book to children (the part that relates to the question or phenomenon of study) is fine to do in STEM education with young children. We don't have to read the entire book, just what we need to know at the time. Later we may want to read the whole book as a way of putting the pieces or process together, but teachers can decide what is and isn't relevant for their young students.

Children engaged in a story-retelling project with the three pigs had an opportunity to build their own houses out of paper and blow them down, exploring how their own huffs and puffs can create force and motion.

Similarly, teachers direct children to understand and retell a portion of a nonfiction book or life cycle, for example, as a way to communicate ideas. In one preschool classroom, the teacher divided the book *How a Plant Grows* into segments and had her small groups retell different parts of the book during the plant project (Kalman 1997). Together the class could tell the story (communicate ideas) of how a plant grows with their own pictures created during each stage of the bean plant's growth.

In the following section, you'll find story-retelling suggestions for children's books connecting with STEM inquiries or studies. Most of the books are fiction, which I recommend as accompanying a STEM study as part of a literacy center or small-group session. Nonfiction books are suggested too and will easily fit into a STEM center or small-group session, providing information to advance children's studies or answer their questions.

When I set up story-retelling centers, I include all props or visual aids, and a copy of the book for children in case they want to reference it during the retelling or enacting experience. When story retelling happens at the sensory table, children often are so engaged with the experience that they move off in their own creative directions with the story line and don't typically think to reference the book. In my opinion, this is fine for the sake of creativity, play, and exploration. On the other hand, teachers can opt to play with children at the sensory table and, through guided play, enact the story "by the book"; then, once the teacher leaves the sensory table, the story can take on its own trajectory. All the same, I like to have a special copy of the book nearby even in the sensory area in case children need to see it. I use clear contact paper for coating the pages (for book longevity) so sand and water and other special sensory things (like ooey-gooey stuff) can be wiped away.

Images of Story Retelling for STEM Connections

STEM Concept: Earth Science—Rocks

Stick and Stone by Beth Ferry, illustrated by Tom Lichtenheld (2015)

Character props are simple to put together, requiring one stick and one smooth, rounded rock. A pinecone may be added for the third character. The setting may be imagined, created with props inside the classroom, placed in the sensory table, or conducted outdoors.

Summary of the Story	Why This Book Has Potential for Story Retelling
This fictional account of characters Stick and Stone tells how they became friends. Later a hurricane blows Stick away (the problem of the story). Stone finds and rescues Stick, and all is well once again.	The sparse text and simple story line, coupled with a problem, make this a good story-retelling activity for young children. I love that children will be using a stone, stick, and pinecone as props.

Vocabulary

- lonely
- alone
- zero
- pinecone
- vanish
- wander
- explore
- laze
- shore
- hurricane
- windblown
- puddle
- muddle
- rescue

Supportive Nonfiction Texts

- *Eyewitness: Rocks and Minerals* by R. F. Symes (2014, paperback edition)
- *If You Find a Rock* by Peggy Christian, photographs by Barbara Hirsch Lember (2008)
- *A Rock Can Be . . .* by Laura Purdie Salas, illustrations by Violeta Dabija (2015)
- *A Rock Is Lively* by Dianna Hutts Aston, illustrated by Sylvia Long (2012)

STEM Connections to the Story

- Earth sciences: rocks, hurricane, beach/sand
- Physical sciences: bubbles
- Life sciences: pinecone, sticks, and trees (Pay attention to the endpapers of this book since they tell a story about how stick and stone came to be.)
- Math: focus on numerals 0, 1, 10

Supportive Poetry

- *A Stick Is an Excellent Thing: Poems Celebrating Outdoor Play* by Marilyn Singer (2012), illustrated by LeUyen Pham (See pp. 28–29 for a delightful poem about the potentials of a stick.)

(continued on next page)

(continued from previous page)

Props/Visual Aids for Story Retelling

- One stick with a leaf attached (I used hot glue to attach a silk leaf near the top of the stick; add eyes and a mouth.)
- One round-shaped stone (Add eyes and a mouth.)
- One small pinecone
- Extra props as desired: A sensory table filled with sand. Put a pan of water in it for the ocean, have a hurricane, then make a puddle for Stick to fall into. Specific settings include a playground with a teeter-totter and a swing set; a small bottle of bubbles; and a beach.

Differentiation Strategies

- Simplify this activity by directing what comes next.
- Teachers can ask children to retell individually if a more challenging experience is desired (I believe this story should be collaboratively told in pairs, however, because it is a friendship story).

Directions

- The story lends itself to enacting with a friend in a sand-filled sensory table. One person could be Stick and another Stone. Use as few or as many extra props as desired. Because his role is small, Pinecone can be represented by one of the two participants or by a third person.
- When reading a second or third time through or while modeling the retelling, teachers should clarify the figurative language with children by asking if they understand what it means to be a zero (referencing social situations). Then ask what numeral the stone looks like. Repeat with the stick character. The figurative and literal language occur in a few places in the book.

Additional Concepts

Social-emotional themes (alone, lonely, friends)

Related STEM Inquiries

- How are rocks the same? How are they different? Investigate the properties of selected rocks and minerals. Moomaw offers extensive ideas in *Teaching STEM in the Early Years* (2013). One activity has children exploring properties of five different rocks and minerals: mica, granite, sandstone, talc, and pumice (36–37).
- What can we learn when we explore rocks? Create a rock collection with the class: go on rock hunts outdoors or ask a rock collector or geologist in your community to visit the class and share a few samples.
- Which rock is heavier? Which is lighter? Pose problems with rocks, such as comparing rocks by weighing them to discover which is heavier or finding out how many pebbles equal one stone on the balance scales.

STEM Concept: Earth Science—Shadows

Moonbear's Shadow by Frank Asch ([1985] 2014)

Some teachers like using this book after children have begun shadow studies so they can have practical opportunities to understand shadow "behavior" prior to reading about it. Others like to offer the book to children before shadow studies to present a discrepant event and kick off the study.

Summary of the Story

Moonbear's shadow frightens a fish away just as he is about to catch it (the problem). Moonbear spends most of the rest of the book trying to get his shadow to disappear. Just when he thought he was rid of it, the shadow reappears. He makes a deal with his shadow, and they catch a fish together in the evening.

Why This Book Has Potential for Story Retelling

The book requires one character and one shadow. Nearly everyone has either a stuffed or plastic bear somewhere to use for Moonbear, so props are fairly easy to gather.

Vocabulary

- fishing pole
- line
- brook
- cliff
- hammer and nails
- shovel
- cast

Supportive Nonfiction Texts

- *Guess Whose Shadow?* by Stephen Swineburne (2002)
- *Shadows and Reflections* by Tana Hoban (1990)
- *What Makes a Shadow?* by Clyde Bulla, illustrated by June Otani (1994)

STEM Connections to the Story

- The story addresses shadow concepts by describing a typical progression of shadows during the day.
- Shadows need a source of light and an object. Shadows occur because the object is blocking the light source.
- Shadows have the general shape of the object the light source is shining on.
- Without a source of light, there is no shadow for the object and vice versa. The angle of the light on the object may produce little to no shadow around noon.

Supportive Poetry

"My Shadow" by Robert Louis Stevenson. The poem is found online or in *A Child's Garden of Verses* by Robert Louis Stevenson, edited by Tasha Tudor (1999, 24). See also *A Poem Is—My Shadow* read by Bill Connolly (a Disney Jr. YouTube video featuring a Peter Pan shadow sequence—the animation explains some of the more challenging vocabulary in the poem, and the reading of it is exquisite: www.youtube.com/watch?v=Ha5Dp2NGFRM).

(continued on next page)

(continued from previous page)

Props/Visual Aids for Story Retelling

- Brown bear toy or stuffed animal
- Flashlight
- Extra props could include a toy shovel, toy hammer and nails, and a little house for the bear to take a nap away from the light source

Differentiation Strategies

- To simplify, provide more teacher support in the form of active directing.
- To make the story-retelling experience more challenging, have children manipulate two or more of these: the flashlight, bear, and story narrative.

Additional Concepts

Addressing Bear's misconception: Bear believes Shadow is a separate entity that makes his or her own decisions. He talks to his shadow and makes a deal. Do we do that with our own shadows? Why or why not?

Directions

- When modeling the retelling with children, use a flashlight. Afterward provide a small-group experience with flashlights and objects. Collect data about shadows, revisit, notice patterns, and document learning.
- Model the story again.
- If needed, provide time for children to further explore flashlights shining on objects to discover and understand how shadows are made, how they can grow and decrease in size, and how positions of the light source and object make a difference on the shadow size and location.
- Make a plan for staging the light source with the story's beginning, middle, and end.
- Have children take turns being the light source and manipulating the flashlight on the toy to discover how the light positions affect shadow length. Use guided play/discovery strategies to assist children with knowing where to place the light so Moonbear has a shadow (or no shadow) in the story.
- With small groups, take turns telling parts of the story or enacting parts until children become more familiar with the story and how to make shadows to correlate with the shadows in the book.

Related STEM Inquiries

These inquiries are based on the Reggio Emilia literature describing a project on shadows: teachers posed questions and children explored their own shadows by tracing them at different times of the day; children investigated the shadows of clay people; and they drew pictures of people and their shadows (Malaguzzi and Petter 1996; Filippini and Vecchi 1996).

- What does my shadow look like? Does my shadow stay the same? Ask a friend to trace your shadow on large black mural paper with white crayon or chalk (use large white paper if black is not available and paint it later). Cut out the shadows and compare them with shadows at different times of the day. Teachers may take photographs of children getting their shadows traced and of children with shadows at different times of the day.
- Do shadows only happen outside? How can we find out? Try children's ideas. Consider manipulating different light sources indoors.

- Make people and animal figures out of clay and find out what happens when we add flashlights or lamps. Consider having children trace the shadow of their clay person or animal as part of their exhibit. Create a drawing of yourself and add your shadow.
- Have children make paper drawings of themselves on card stock. Cut out the pictures and use a base (precut) to stand the figures up (like standing paper dolls with a paper base inserted). Create shadows with a lamp, then trace the shadows on black paper. Cut the shadows out and tape it to the bases of the paper doll characters.

STEM Concept: Life Sciences—Birds

Feathers for Lunch by Lois Ehlert (1990)

Two supportive structures for retelling: a clothesline for pinning up visual aids in sequence, and plush cat and bird props.

Summary of the Story

A cat seeks birds to eat for lunch, but the closest he can get are feathers for lunch because his wise owner put a warning bell on him.

Supplemental Fiction/Concept Book

- *Birds* by Kevin Henkes, illustrated by Laura Dronzek (2009). This lovely book is designed for very young children and will capture their interests and imaginations.

Vocabulary

- spicy
- tame
- mild
- wild
- snooping
- sneaking
- warning
- soar
- prowling
- munch

STEM Connections to the Story

- Birds and differences among birds as noted in the art
- Feathers
- Cats as predators
- Habitat

Why This Book Has Potential for Story Retelling

This book explores the concept of a cat just missing when he tries to catch a bird to eat for lunch. Implied is the concept of predators in the natural world. Ehlert creates the birds on each page as life-sized; she also offers interesting information about the birds and flowers throughout the book and a simple (and most appreciated) field guide of sorts in the back of the book.

Supportive Nonfiction Texts

- *Birdsongs* by Betsy Franco and Steve Jenkins (2007)
- *Eyewitness: Bird* by David Burnie (2008)

Supportive Poetry

- *Read-Aloud Rhymes for the Very Young* by Jack Prelutsky, illustrated by Marc Brown (1986), contains four bird poems.

(continued on next page)

(continued from previous page)

Props/Visual Aids for Story Retelling

Props

- Use a plush cat and plush Audubon birds (with authentic birdcalls recorded by the Cornell Lab of Ornithology inside that activate when pressed).
- Tie a large jingle bell around the cat's neck.
- Add colored craft feathers to the mix so the cat can be left with feathers when the bird flies away.

Visual Aids

- Either cut out "The Lunch That Got Away" bird pictures at the back of a spare copy of the book or find images of real birds. Number the backs of the cards in order of appearance in the story and laminate them on card stock. You will need an American robin, blue jay, northern cardinal, house wren, red-headed woodpecker, red-winged blackbird, northern oriole, mourning dove, northern flicker, ruby-throated hummingbird, house sparrow, and American goldfinch.
- Cut a good cat face out of the nonusable book or find a cat picture to serve as the cat in the retelling. Mount on card stock and laminate.
- Using a clothesline, pin the birds in order for children's early retellings. Add a colored feather most representative of the bird to the base of each card for the cat to pick up when he visits each bird.
- See Recommended Resources for additional information.

Differentiation Strategies

- To simplify, narrate the story for children and scaffold the retelling experience as needed; let groups of children retell the story, each taking on a role of a bird or the cat.
- To make the retelling more challenging, have children put the birds in sequence and retell the story themselves; later consider asking children to identify the birds if interest ensues.

Directions

- While retelling the story, have the cat visit each bird on the line in sequence, jump at the bird, then let the bird fly away and come back with a feather.
- If using plush birds with birdcalls, have each child be one of the birds. The children can fly away and make their calls. Ehlert's book includes the birdcalls for each as extra information on each page.

Additional Concepts

Feathers, nests, eggs, what different birds eat, pets, wild versus tame, animal needs, flowers

Related STEM Activities

- How do feathers feel? How are they the same or different? What is the function of feathers? The book draws out the attributes of feathers, so this is a good area of focus for an inquiry project. Purchase natural feathers from craft stores (rather than using found feathers) to observe with magnifying glasses or child-safe microscopes.
- What do different birds eat? Consider a responsible way to have a bird feeder outside a classroom window for ongoing, year-round observations; find out what different birds eat in the wild.
- How does each bird sound? Are there patterns in their calls? When we help children listen to and differentiate sounds in nature, we are supporting skills that help them hear the sounds in words. Use the Audubon plush birds to help children identify patterns and birdcalls outdoors when they play. See Moomaw for more (2013, 112–14).

STEM Concept: Life Sciences—Insects

The Very Quiet Cricket by Eric Carle (1990)

This story-retelling visual aid was made from photographs of the real animals that were pasted to cardboard puzzle pieces cut so that only the correct pieces fit together, making it self-checking.

Summary of the Story

A little cricket is born but is quiet. The cricket is greeted by many insects but cannot respond in kind until the end of the story when the cricket has grown and found a friend.

Why This Book Has Potential for Story Retelling

This fictional story is linear in that the cricket meets various insects along the way toward maturity and finds a friend at the end. Repetitive text is helpful in retelling. Remembering the sequence could be problematic because there are so many insects to meet. Confusing the sequence really doesn't change the story, however, so I wouldn't get too hung up on order until much later in the story-retelling experience.

Vocabulary

- chirped
- whizzed
- locust
- spinning
- praying mantis
- crunched, munched
- bubbled
- spittlebug
- slurping
- screeched
- cicada
- bumble bee
- whirred
- dragonfly
- gliding
- luna moth
- sailed
- stillness
- silently
- chirped

Supportive Nonfiction Texts

- *Eyewitness: Insect* by Laurence Mound (2007)

STEM Connections to the Story

- The STEM value in this book is in meeting insects through Carle's expressionistic style. They are common insects, and children likely will come across a few examples at home or at school.
- The idea of insect communication is implied. We hear a cricket sound at the end. How might we consider listening to the sounds of the other insects in the book?

Supportive Poetry

- "Crickets" by Valerie Worth in *The Random House Book of Poetry for Children* edited by Jack Prelutsky, illustrated by Arnold Lobel (1983, 73)

(continued on next page)

(continued from previous page)

Props/Visual Aids for Story Retelling

- Find pictures of the insects and print them on card stock in color.
- Cut them out and mount them on colored paper to make them stronger. I mounted my pictures on card stock that was cut out in a generic puzzle piece. I then put them in book order and cut unique puzzle edges so only the correct piece would fit.
- Number the back of the insect pictures according to their sequence of appearance to serve as a self-checking mechanism for children who understand number sequence.
- Laminate the pictures to make them durable.
- See Recommended Resources for additional information.

Directions

- Encourage children to say the repeating phrase in the book while retelling the story.

Differentiation Strategies

- In early retellings, children may not remember the names of insects. To simplify, just have children greet the insect if they don't know the insect's name.
- To further simplify, put puzzle pieces together to create a linear storyboard for the child to take the sequencing variable out of the retelling. Have the little cricket puzzle piece then follow a linear sequence to the end of the story.
- To challenge students further, have them name each insect the little cricket meets and conduct the sequencing themselves.

Additional Concepts

Insect sounds, how insects make their sounds, what insects look like up close, insect behavior

Related STEM Activities

- What do our crickets like to eat? *Creepy Crawlies and the Scientific Method* by Sally Kneidel is a terrific resource for teachers who recognize the joy of having a pet insect in the classroom (2015). Kneidel notes that a cricket can live quite nicely on moistened bread, damp Cheerios, carrot sections, lettuce, water droplets sprayed in the terrarium, and about two inches of sand on the floor. Children can do simple experiments by putting one known preferred food and another type of food in the terrarium and observing to see the crickets' culinary preferences. Children can make observational drawings and participate in collecting data.
- Do insects in the book sound like the words used by author Eric Carle? The sounds made by insects can be found online for children to hear at centers or small-group time.

STEM Concept: Physics—The Function and Properties of Wheels Using Force

Duck on a Bike by David Shannon (2002)

This delightful story is fun to retell with animal toys and pretend bicycles created to cover a standard block.

Summary of the Story

Duck rides a bike and greets farm animals, each of whom greets him with respect—yet their thoughts are either concerning or judgmental. The moment the farm animals get a chance to ride themselves, however, they do so. They return the bikes before they are missed, so none of the owners realize what happened.

Why This Book Has Potential for STEM Retelling

The story line appeals to children, and is simple, repetitive, and ends with a humorous tone.

Supportive Fiction

- *Cars and Trucks and Things That Go* by Richard Scarry (1998)

Vocabulary

- farm
- duck
- waddled
- parked
- wobbled
- cow
- sheep
- dog
- trick
- cat
- pedaled
- horse
- chicken
- goat
- pig
- show-off
- mouse
- bunch

Supportive Nonfiction

- *What Do Wheels Do All Day?* by April Jones Prince, illustrated by Giles Laroche (2006)
- *What Is a Wheel and Axle?* by Lloyd Douglas (2002)

STEM Connections to the Story

- At the beginning of the story, the bike wobbled because duck was going slowly. Questions could be asked about this situation in the book, leading toward rolling a small wheel with weak force followed by rolling a wheel with strong force and noticing changes.

Supportive Poetry or Song

- *The Wheels on the Bus* by Paul O. Zelinsky (1990). This version is a popular pop-up book; several versions are in print.

(continued on next page)

(continued from previous page)

Props/Visual Aids for Story Retelling

- Plastic farm animals. You will need a duck, cow, sheep, dog, cat, horse, chicken, goat, two pigs, and one small mouse.
- 10 pretend bicycles made out of heavy paper and laminated for plastic animals to ride. If you want the pigs to ride a bicycle built for two, you'll have to create one separately for them and will only need eight total bicycles instead.
- The setting is a farm, so a red barn and fencing should be included if you have them.

Differentiation Strategies

- To simplify, assign one animal to each child in the group. This will allow children to learn their animal's response to Duck. When it is their turn next time, they may select another animal if they wish.
- To challenge children, provide them with several animal parts to play.

Directions

- Using the props, retell the story in sequence.

Additional Concepts

Farm animals, fiction (fantasy farm animal behavior) versus nonfiction (real farm animal behavior)

Related STEM Activities

- What is common to all wheels? What is the function of wheels? Read *What Do Wheels Do All Day?* Make a collection of wheels (old toy wheels that are wide are particularly nice for rolling with some force behind them). Put them in the sensory table or take them outside to make track impressions outdoors. Investigate small and large forces on wheels and their responses. What else affects the way a wheel rolls?
- What happens when we push, pull, pedal, tow, stroll, and roll wheels? Investigate vocabulary words by trying them out with different pushing, pulling, and riding toys (gross motor toys). Another day, try it with smaller cars and trucks and other things that go. Collect children's observations (to help you remember to ask children about them during meeting and to document the study and their language).
- Are wheels able to roll without us giving them force?
- What do wheels do for us? Go on a wheel observation walk. Tell which wheels you see while walking and what those wheels are doing for people.

STEM Concept: Mathematics—Spatial Relationships, Composing, and Decomposing

Changes, Changes by Pat Hutchins (1987)

Using natural wood blocks takes the color variable out of replication. The book contains block structures that may be imitated but not precisely replicated. Exploring why this is so makes for an interesting analysis.

Summary of the Story

This classic wordless picture book shares the story of a block man and woman who build a home, and after it catches on fire, they build a fire engine to put out the fire. The story continues with transformations from fire engine to a boat (it appears they used too much water for the fire), and several more constructions before ending back where we started, with a house. In this regard, the book is a circle book.

Why This Book Has Potential for Story Retelling

The book lends itself to constructing while retelling—which is perfect for STEM retellings and makes for interesting analysis when exact replication of the structures is not possible.

Vocabulary

This is a wordless picture book, so teachers encourage the vocabulary of construction, geometry, positional words in space, and spatial relationships in their descriptive telling, retelling, and questions.

Supportive Nonfiction Texts

- *Dreaming Up: A Celebration of Building* by Christy Hale. This book is an absolute must as a companion book. Each spread features a painting of multicultural children building with materials. On the opposite page is a photograph of a building (international focus) looking much like the child's construction. The back matter of the book offers information about each authentic building to share with children if interest prevails.

STEM Connections to the Story

- Constructing and deconstructing
- Geometry
- Spatial relationships
- Positional words in space

Supportive Poetry

- "Construction" by Lilian Moore, in *A Jar of Tiny Stars: Poems by NCTE Award-Winning Poets*, edited by Bernice Cullinan.

(continued on next page)

(continued from previous page)

Props/Visual Aids for Story Retelling

Colored blocks are depicted in the book, but be aware that if trying to replicate the colors, children may not have access to orange arches. I recommend natural wood blocks to take the color variables out of the picture. Children may wish to use colored blocks but should be advised that their color selections likely won't match the pictures. Try to have enough blocks for each child to create a construction from the book.

Directions

- With small-group work, each child may imitate one of the constructions in the book, then retell the story as a group when finished. Note that replication is not possible for all pictures due to wheels and some of the arch shapes.
- Wordless picture books can be a little more work for teachers than reading text. First, either coconstruct the story with children (think of good questions to ask ahead of time) or think of the story, expressions, and vocabulary ahead of time, tailoring the story to meet the pictures but also to meet children's interests and vocabulary needs.
- An alternative method for retelling is to deconstruct an old copy of the book and create story-retelling visual aids out of the pictures, encouraging children to use their words when retelling.
- Plan for a space or tabletop construction and allow for sequential construction of the story on the table for retelling in stages.

Differentiation Strategies

- To simplify the retelling, break the story into segments and provide one portion to each child during small-group work; help children understand their roles in constructing then telling the story of why the construction had to be made.
- To challenge children, consider asking them to create names for the people in the story and add details about their move.

Additional Concepts

Transportation vehicles, emergency vehicles, fire, putting out a fire (the book may go well with a fire safety unit; "stop, drop, and roll" could be practiced in the story)

Related STEM Activity

How can you plan to build your next structure? Ask children to design their own structures and then build them. *Changes, Changes* enables children to imitate structures from a model presented in the book. We know that the work of engineers is to design and build. In *Building Structures with Young Children*, Chalufour and Worth suggest that children have experiences with sketching their own block structures (2004). Consider asking children to draw a plan prior to building, create the plan, and compare their constructions to their plans. Why were changes made? Relate changes to why the structures children built to imitate the structures in *Changes, Changes* were different from those shown in the book.

STEM Concept: Technology—The Way Things Work

Alexander and the Wind-Up Mouse by Leo Lionni ([1969] 1987)

Alexander and the Wind-Up Mouse can serve as a motivator for a STEM study into how wind-up toys work.

Summary of the Story

Alexander is a lonely, underappreciated mouse until he meets Willy, a wind-up mouse belonging to the little girl who lives in the house with her parents. When Willy gets cast aside, Alexander makes a wish and gets it in the end.

Why This Book Has Potential for Story Retelling

The story has a clear story line that captivates young children. It has an element of magic and includes a piece of technology: a wind-up mouse.

Vocabulary

- wind-up
- lizard
- magic
- pebble

Supportive Nonfiction Texts

- *The Way Things Work Now* by David Macauley (2016, 78–81). This book addresses how springs work, which is fundamental to how the wind-up mouse works (we wind up the spring inside to make it move). Macaulay's words and illustrations show how springs work.

STEM Connections to the Story

- The story raises the question of how things work.

Supportive Poetry

- *Mice* by Rose Fyleman, illustrated by Lois Ehlert (2012)

Props/Visual Aids for Story Retelling

- One mouse finger puppet
- At least one wind-up mouse (extras for playing or centers-based disassembly)
- One colorful lizard
- A purple pebble

Directions

- Enact or retell the story with props. Few, if any, setting props will be needed.

Differentiation Strategies

- To simplify the story-retelling experience, keep a copy of the book nearby for reference; break the story into shorter segments and support with hints.
- To make the story more challenging for children, provide them with longer segments to retell and hold back on helping until it is requested.

Additional Concepts

Mice, care of mice, how things work

(continued on next page)

(continued from previous page)

Related STEM Activities

- How does a wind-up mouse work? What is inside a wind-up mouse? Macaulay's 2016 *The Way Things Work Now* offers insight into how springs work. Taking apart a wind-up mouse requires a small sewing machine screwdriver and a small clear container for storing and later viewing or exploring parts. If this is the first time to take a wind-up toy apart with children, teachers might model in front of children as a group exploration of the parts and what's inside, keeping a container nearby for the parts and for passing them around to everyone to observe. Otherwise, teachers and children may take apart wind-up mice together in small groups with one screwdriver, mouse, and container per child. Have extra mice around for playing, because once taken apart, they likely won't go back together again. The wind-up toys include a small-parts warning, so placing the pieces in a clear bag or container for viewing and exploration purposes is a great idea.

- Describe what we found inside the wind-up mouse. Make a drawing of what is inside the wind-up mouse. How does your new drawing differ from your first drawing?

- What else might we take apart? Create an "exploration station" in your classroom for safely deconstructing things that no longer work (broken toys that cannot be fixed or electronic toys are a good start). Always check for safety and use safety goggles before deconstructing. For young children in particular, cut off the plugs, check for very sharp parts and small parts, and pull tubes and especially old batteries out of the parts ahead of time. Proceed with safety and adult supervision.

- Create an ECE "makers space" center in your classroom for inventing and creating with old (safe) parts, recyclables, and donated materials.

Making Number Sense with Story Retelling

Story retelling is a strategy to support the language of math and especially number sense. In both story retelling and the development of number sense, teachers facilitate language development and conceptual understanding. We provide young children with props or manipulatives as representational objects in both story retelling and mathematics learning. In both areas, children play active roles in learning. Because of the nature of children's learning through exploration, experience, play, and manipulation of objects, story retelling and the development of number sense go hand in hand. Breaking down the big idea of number sense serves as a good starting point for matching good books to key concepts.

While working with a small group in an early retelling episode, this teacher candidate focused on simple concepts: counting and one-to-one correspondence (while ignoring the math problems during the retelling session). Doing so enabled her to conduct an informal assessment before moving to teacher-supported enactments of the math problems in later retellings.

Developing Number Sense for Mathematizing the World

Math is all around us, and helping children "see" the math in our indoor and outdoor environments assists them in understanding more difficult concepts later. Finding a circle in a flowerpot, a line in a sidewalk, or a square in the school windowpanes is a way of making math connections to the world. If we talk about corners when the opportunity arrives—as noticed in books, tables, window sills, and where the wall meets the ceiling or floor—children will have a reference point for understanding shapes, angles, and, later, geometric reasoning. When we line up and count children, then later use the vocabulary of first, second, third, and so on, we are mathematizing our preschool environments. Developing the vocabulary of mathematics is essential in the early years.

Before they really understand the concept of numbers, children typically memorize the sequence of number words. Very young children are quite adept at memorization, and if parents or caregivers provide children with experiences in counting—for example, counting steps as they walk up to the third-floor apartment, then counting again as they walk down—children will eventually count along and soon be able to count alone. Memorizing numbers, like memorizing the alphabet, is useful to children, their parents, and teachers because it serves as a starting point to teach number concepts.

Early Math Concepts

Before children develop number sense, they must develop early concepts, skills, and vocabulary. The National Council of Teachers of Mathematics (NCTM) and the National Association for the Education of Young Children (NAEYC) created a joint position statement in 2010 on the importance of having a carefully considered math curriculum for young children because the early childhood years serve as building blocks for later math success. Early concepts in matching, classifying, comparing, and ordering objects, for example, play strongly into developing number sense. For more, NCTM (2009) and Smith (2013) offer detailed accounts on how to approach these topics with young children from a developmental perspective.

One early math concept necessary to acquiring number sense is matching—which really is all about one-to-one correspondence. Young children can informally learn matching while setting the table, putting one napkin on each placemat and placing one cup near each plate. Each child has his or her own cubby at school, gets one snack portion, and receives one heart-shaped cookie during the Valentine's Day party—all examples of one-to-one correspondence. Teachers intentionally provide young children with opportunities to match small sets of objects before moving to more complex one-to-one endeavors.

Comparison and its related vocabulary, such as *big, little, large, small, fast, slow*, and so on, is another early math concept. Comparison words help children when they classify objects—when children place objects in similar attribute groups or sets, which is helpful to young children because number essentially

After reading *A Pair of Socks* (Murphy 2006), this teacher candidate asked children to match real pairs of socks and also asked them to draw a matching pair of socks as a preassessment strategy to check children's understanding of matching. Understanding the concept of matching is necessary in retelling this simple story successfully.

is in reference to a set of objects. Classifying is another early math concept that is learned without necessarily having a developed sense of number.

Additional early math-related vocabulary includes positional words in space: *in*, *out*, *apart*, *over*, *under*, and so on. Teachers set up math environments and scenarios that help children enact these words and reinforce vocabulary. Children also learn directional words: *up*, *down*, *around*, and *forward*, for example. They learn the vocabulary of sequence—from smallest to largest, from thinnest to thickest, or from shortest to tallest. Sequencing skills are necessary in understanding seriation or ordering.

Early math concepts cannot be learned in isolation. Intentionality in teaching and in communicating (or interacting) with children is required. We are in a position of interpreting the mathematical world to children, and our opportunities are rich, indeed.

This child refers to the book *Five Little Pumpkins* as her teacher reads to her. She arranges pumpkins as she learns how to retell the fingerplay story in sequence.

Number Sense Concepts

Just as informal experiences play into the development of early math concepts, so, too, do they play into the development of number sense. When children understand one-to-one correspondence, they are able to associate one number word with one object. If they acquired stable order rule, where the order of the number words in counting always remains the same, they are rote counting. Putting one-to-one correspondence and stable order together enables the child to count objects accurately. She is able to touch one object in a set, assign it an accurate number word, and go to the next object. When she comes to the last object in the set, however, there is a need for an additional concept to finish the counting. She needs to learn that the number word referencing the last object counted is the number representing the set. Connecting number words to quantities is known as *cardinality.*

Concepts of counting include two additional key principles. First, children develop an understanding that anything in a set can be counted as part of the number set. In other words, the objects can be all the same—counting crayons; or they can be different—counting crayons *and* finger puppets, or counting a set of five different objects. The knowledge that any object in a collection can be counted is called the *abstraction principle.* Second, a successful counting experience requires children to know that the sequence of counting objects in a set does not matter as long as they count each object just one time. Knowing that objects can be counted in any order is the *order-irrelevance principle.*

Fingerplays, Number Rhymes, Poems, Songs, and Chants

A long line of fingerplays, poems, songs, and chants (including several attributed to Mother Goose) promotes counting and number sense in the early years. Just about any counting rhyme or fingerplay may be found online. *Marc Brown's Playtime Rhymes: A Treasury for Families to Learn and Play Together* is the third book Brown has produced in this genre and includes several counting rhymes (2013). I love these books because Brown illustrates the fingerplay concept or story along with illustrations of the fingerplay movements next to the words. Our number system is a base-ten system, and many of our early fingerplays begin in fives and move toward complexity in addressing the concept of ten. Conveniently, our fingers and hands help us learn sets of five. With five on each hand, our ten fingers are assets to children in understanding our number system.

Early experiences with number rhymes and fingerplays can be supported with children's books and actually explored beyond the book when props are included. Using finger puppets is a nice way to make the rhymes come alive. We turn fingers into one little duck, two little pumpkins, three fat turkeys, four little bunnies, or five little snowmen. In small groups, each child can represent one of something in a group retelling. In addition, with math fingerplays, it's not only good counting practice to learn the fingerplay and retell or sing and enact, it's also really a great idea to explore or play with materials and number.

In the developmental trajectory discussed in chapter 4, we considered that children start with whole concepts; in the case of the fingerplays, we are generally talking about the number concept of five (the whole). Such fingerplays typically lose one monkey (who fell off the bed), with a remaining set of fingers left (until none remain), which is a subtraction concept. Alternatively, the fingerplay may build up to five (adding on by one) or it may actually be a combination of taking away one at a time, then adding them back at the end, such as with *Five Little Ducks*. Using props such as

After practice with their own fingers and puppets, and making their frog headbands, children enact the fingerplay story.

finger puppets or construction-paper headbands to enact adding or taking away is another way to represent the story and build math concepts through experience.

Focusing on One Number Set

Books that address only one number set are helpful for exploring numbers, one set at a time. *Rabbit Pie* explores the concept of six with a significant amount of matching sets included: six carrots, six cups, and so on (Ives 2006). Using books that focus on one number set at a time can offer children an opportunity to pause and explore the properties of the number and its associated written numeral.

Counting Books

Counting books are usually considered concept books. The concept of counting is addressed, and then the book ends. However, some do have stories woven into the counting. One of the largest benefits of counting books is that they give children the opportunity to visualize multiple quantities in groups or sets and compare. Counting books offer potential to explore number through pictures.

Counting books are unidirectional (either counting forward or counting backward) and also bidirectional (counting forward and backward). Most counting books describe and count different sets of objects (one fish, two ants, three dogs), leading toward a significant buildup of different props or visual aids. You might think that story retelling with this type of counting book requires you to collect fifty-five total items representing ten different things, but not so. Instead, when using a counting book with different sets for retelling in the math manipulatives center, teachers often include a tubful of cubes, encouraging children to represent each number with the cubes as they move through a counting book, which provides hands-on experiences with number concepts. Because there isn't much of a story to tell, the value in representing the objects using cubes is that it is a more symbolic level of operating.

Materials are particularly easy to find and inexpensive (they are carnival toys and birthday prizes), and piñatas are fun to fill. This story and materials can spark a store center in the classroom and/or supplement a cultural study quite nicely.

Some counting books address one simple set, often counted from one to ten. Books that address counting one set of objects work well for story retelling with young children mostly because we can get by in the props department by collecting only ten of one type of object. Some counting books count by twos, threes, fours, fives, and so on while others rhyme and others could be considered as works of art. Nicest of all for story retelling are those counting books with a story line, weak though it may be. One counting book with a story line that comes to mind is *Fiesta!* (Guy 2007). The characters in the story prepare for a fiesta that requires a piñata, and they go to the market to purchase toys and candy. They collect up to seven sets, so the number of items for teachers to collect is manageable. In this retelling experience, we always sort the toys back into their containers at the end so they are ready to go for the next retelling.

Tana Hoban has been creating books addressing STEM themes for more than thirty years. *Let's Count* is a particularly wonderful book for young children that needs no additional props (1999). Hoban's photography in this book demonstrates the number sets in the real world. Hoban uses one page of the spread to designate the numeral, the dot array, and the number word. The second page is dedicated to the photograph of the number set. Her nearly wordless picture book takes us into the world of three holes, four balloons, and five crushed soda cans. Children and teachers alike love her books.

Part-Whole Relationships

Children who are in pre-K need experiences in part-whole relationships. The part-whole relationship concept refers to the ability to take numbers apart into smaller sets and have the awareness that those smaller sets (the parts) together equal the whole. In other words, the number in the whole set does not change just by splitting it apart. This concept also teaches children that there are lots of different ways to represent one number. Readiness for part-whole relationships is contingent on children's understanding of counting and composition of sets. Nelson offers math games and ideas for teaching young children about key number sense concepts and describes how teachers might recognize when children are ready for part-whole relationships, around the age of four (2007, 111). This occurs when they (a) understand that objects, when rearranged in a set, remain the same number (they don't recount); (b) can count forward and backward at different numbers (other than one); (c) can count on to find the differences between two numbers; and (d) can determine the missing part of a whole by knowing one part of the whole.

If we use a children's book such as Robert McCloskey's *Make Way for Ducklings* (1941) as a way to explore part-whole relationships (in this case, with the duckling characters in the book), we are mathematizing the book, going beyond the story and into an extension, which is a great way to look at sets and break them into parts. Using props to support beginning part-whole relationships means we explore the nature of a number—let's say five—by manipulating five objects into two or more sets. Five is composed of the sets five and zero, four and one, three and two, two and three, one and four, and, finally, zero and five. But five also includes more than just two sets of objects. Five can be five sets of one. Five can also be broken into two sets of two and one set of one, and so on. When teachers help children discover these different combinations, they are helping children gather a strong sense of number, beneficial to adding and subtracting later. All of these combinations of sets make up a set of five (sometimes called the five family with children).

Part-whole relationships can be found in stories. One great example is *The Poky Little Puppy* by Janette Sebring Lowrey (2001). It addresses the part-whole concept of five by repeating a scenario over and over again that shares the story of five puppies that split into two sets: four puppies and one poky little puppy. The part-whole relationship repeats in the narrative and also in Gustaf Tenggren's illustrations, not only when the puppies go out into the world each new day, but also when they come home to eat dinner and go to sleep.

A teacher who uses *The Poky Little Puppy* for retelling with young children will find that its repeating lines and predictable structure lend toward successful retelling experience for the child who has some experience in retelling familiar tales, songs, or fingerplays. Before retelling, teachers explore concepts of the recurring problem and final solution to the story, and vocabulary such as *poky*, *lizard*, and *rice pudding*. Checking for understanding of the part-whole relationship addressed in the book is needed for retelling with meaning.

Teachers might consider exploring part-whole relationships for the number five with puppy finger puppets. Teachers make up scenarios and act them out with children and props: "Pretend that only three puppies went up the hill; how many stayed back at the bottom of the hill, sniffing at the ground? How many puppies are there?" Then act it out with puppy finger puppets or, better yet, with the children themselves. Wilburne, Keat, and Napoli, and Whitin and Whitin recommend mathematizing children's literature to explore and practice math concepts, and the experience can only provide deeper understanding (2011; 2004).

Finding books that express one number set in part-whole relationships is a little tricky but is possible. *Five Creatures* addresses part-whole relationships when the five creatures that live in a house (two adults, one child, and two cats) are separated into parts that equal five (by attributes) at the beginning and end of the book (Jenkins 2005). Near the middle of the book, however, the author focuses on attributes only and abandons the part-whole relationship of the set of five. The switch in focus might be okay for older students but could be confusing to young children when trying to center on part-whole relationships for the number five using this book. Following this section, I suggest an activity with *Quack and Count*, which takes a set of seven ducks and breaks them into different part-whole relationships with engaging and supportive illustrations (Baker 1999).

Number and Numerals

Children in pre-K are expected to experience numerals—those symbols that represent the number of objects in a set, the number of candles on a birthday cake, or the number of crayons in a box. Associating the numeral with the number of objects is also an informal math learning experience. When we go to a birthday party to celebrate our friend's seventh birthday, the numeral 7 may be on napkins, a candle, or perhaps on other environmental print. In addition, children see nominals in the environment—numerals that describe or represent something such as an address or a phone number. Finally, ordinals—the vocabulary that designates order such as first, second, third, and so on—are useful for young children to learn once they secure the sense of number.

In the story-song *Old MacDonald Had a Farm*, the animals appear in order. This serves as a good opportunity to mathematize the story by attaching the vocabulary of ordinals to the animals after the retelling (or in this case, resinging) of the story.

NCTM recommends that fours and pre-Ks learn to read numerals from 1 to 10 (2009, 2010). Books that focus on numerals in a playful or visually appealing way are useful in supporting numeral identification skills with young children. Typical counting books are terrific, but even more helpful are books that focus on the numbers themselves, helping children recognize and write numerals. One such book, an atypical counting book, is *Numbers* by Sarah Anderson (2009). This book is a highly colorful, artistic, wordless, sturdy concept board book primarily designed for toddlers but a great pick for preschoolers if you want to focus on the concept of number. In addition to the art, I love two things about *Numbers* that make it different from the typical counting book. First, its structure is that of a step book; each page, when turned, reveals a larger page underneath, so when the book is closed, only the numerals 1–10 and title are visible to the reader, allowing children to focus on one number and its set at a time. The step book format entices children to select a number out of numeric order to experience. Again, a focus on number predominates over counting. Second, Anderson included not only the numeral and number of objects on each page, but also the appropriate number of dots (the dot array) to represent each number.

Another book, *What Comes in 2's, 3's, and 4's*, centers only on those particular number sets—it doesn't address counting (Aker 1990). The numerals play a predominant role in the book, but so do the sets. It's a unique book.

Counting On

Children in preschool and kindergarten need time and intentional learning experiences with the number core and manipulatives so that they develop a deep conceptual understanding of number sense. Children who are four and five years old are expected to look at a 5-group (fingers or dot arrays) and count on (NCTM 2010). Teachers who are developing young children's number sense look for books that include dot arrays alongside the pictures, because the representation of quantity in dots is a step in the symbolic ladder between the picture (iconic) and the number (symbolic). The dot array is an easier symbol to understand than the numeral, yet more symbolic than the picture. Giving children exposure to and experience with dot arrays helps them learn to recognize numbers without counting.

Having a multitude of experiences with five little ducks, five green and speckled frogs, five fat turkeys, and five little monkeys coupled with breaking those little sets down into parts and putting them all back together again to make a whole, plus having experiences in seeing sets represented with dot arrays, helps children subitize. When children subitize, they recognize how many are in the 5-group without counting. Subitizing is helpful for counting on. When we count on, we recognize the part—the set of five—in the dot array of seven, then we count "six, seven" to find out how many are in the whole set.

One interesting book that uses dot arrays with number and numerals is Eric Carle's sturdy board book, *My Very First Book of Numbers* (1974). This useful book is actually something of a game. The reader picks a number on the top of the page, then finds the same number of fruit in a picture on the bottom of the page. Each numeral at the top of the page includes a square-dot array to demonstrate number—a very clever little game and interactive book!

Number sense stands as one key foundation for advanced mathematics understanding. Providing young children with meaningful number sense activities through hands-on, language-rich experiences is crucial for developing deep concepts necessary for later academic success.

Story Retelling for Developing Number Sense

Number Sense Concepts: Focusing on the Number 4, Related Numerals, and Counting Backward

Pete the Cat and His Four Groovy Buttons by Eric Litwin, illustrated by James Dean (2012)

Create simple shirts out of bright yellow poster paper, then add four large buttons backed with Velcro. Children use this prop for retelling the story first with the teacher in small groups, then in choice time in the math center.

Summary of the Story

Pete the cat has a beautiful yellow shirt with four groovy buttons—but he loses them all.

Why This Book Has Potential for Story Retelling

The simple rhyming and repetitive text are appealing to children and support the retellings. Additionally, the number concept is low to support successful countdowns.

Vocabulary

- groovy
- favorite
- round
- buttons
- zero
- one
- two
- three
- four
- popped
- rolled
- last
- buttonless

Number Sense Concepts Addressed in the Story

- The number set: four
- Counting backward
- Numerals 0–4
- Number operations (subtraction)

Props/Visual Aids for Story Retelling

- Yellow card stock for child-sized shirts and yellow poster paper for a large shirt for the teacher or a group to use
- Four large buttons per shirt: teal, dark blue, green, and red
- Four large construction paper buttons for the teacher model
- Velcro
- Black marker to outline shirt details

Directions

- Cut out multiple small yellow shirts (enough for each person in small group to have one), and a larger version to serve as a model.
- Outline shirt details with a black marker.
- Place Velcro dots where buttons should appear and add the verso of the Velcro spot to each button.
- Place buttons on the shirts in the same order found in the book.
- Retell the story with children, enacting with the shirts and buttons along the way.

(continued on next page)

(continued from previous page)

Differentiation Strategies

- To simplify the retelling process, have a recording of the story playing during the first few times children participate with the props.
- To create a more challenging retelling, add numerals to the retelling props (0-1-2-3-4) for children to apply when appropriate. A few children may be interested in the number sentences found in the book; if extra challenging material is desired, create a few number sentences for children to apply, just as in the book.

Additional Concepts

Resilience/carrying on (Pete never cries over a missing button and moves on while singing.)

Sparking Exploratory Play (What would happen if . . . ?)

- . . . Pete the Cat opened a button shop? Would someone come to buy some buttons? Who?
- . . . Pete the Cat invited his friends over for a picnic and surfing?

Number Sense Concepts: Focusing on One Number Set and Counting Backward

Five Little Ducks by Penny Ives (2007)

This photo shows two ways to retell the story. Another (not pictured) is to use a blue tub, water, and rubber duckies.

Summary of the Story

Five ducklings go out with their mother and only four return. Each day, Mother Duck loses a duckling until no ducks are left to go outside with her. She goes to the pond anyway, and all five of her little ducklings return home with her for a happy ending.

Why This Book Has Potential for Story Retelling

This familiar fingerplay song has repetitive, predictable, rhyming lines. Children likely will have the song memorized. Because the story lends itself to successful retelling, opportunities to teach and assess math concepts and song vocabulary may be helpful in determining what children are, in fact, understanding about the math concepts and story meaning.

Vocabulary

- hills
- far away
- wandering

Number Sense Concepts Addressed in the Story

- Set of five
- Counting down

(Note that no numerals are present in this particular version of *Five Little Ducks*.)

(continued on next page)

(continued from previous page)

Props/Visual Aids for Story Retelling

- Five duckling finger puppets and one mother duck puppet
- Or five rubber ducklings, a larger rubber duck to play the mother role, and a pan of water so they may float. The narrator can play the mother duck if need be.
- Or cut paper ducks out of yellow card stock and write a numeral just under a wing that folds down; add the dot array visibly (or vice versa: make the dot array hidden and the numeral visible—see photograph)

Directions

- Enact the story with props or visual aids.
- Add complexity to later retellings by giving children the ducks with dot arrays on their feathers and numerals under their wings. These paper ducklings serve as a guess-the-numeral-that-goes-with-the-dot-array game for children when they are not engaged in retelling. If the child chooses to retell with the dot-array ducklings, coach her to "lose" the highest numbered duckling, because this way, the highest number in the group remaining will accurately represent the number of ducklings left.

Differentiation Strategies

- To simplify the activity, scaffold children in taking a duckling away when needed. Consider using the CD that comes with the book in the listening center to support children's decision making, learning, and singing or retelling.
- To make this more challenging, add (1) the dot arrays to match to the set of ducklings with Mother Duck, (2) the numerals (0–5) for children to add to the remaining props when the number of ducklings changes, and/or (3) identification of part-whole relationships for the set of five (for ducks who disappeared and those who remain with Mother Duck).

Additional Concepts

Duck habitats

Sparking Exploratory Play (What would happen if . . . ?)

- . . . the ducklings brought a friend home with them? Who would the friend be? If each of the five ducklings brought a friend home, how many animals would there be altogether?

Number Sense Concept: Number Sets (1-2-3)

Two Mice by Sergio Ruzzier (2015)

Simple mouse headbands are made by either teachers (pictured) or children and serve as costumes for retelling.

Summary of the Story

The story starts with two mice at home, waking up and having cookies together. They go on an adventure that turns a bit dangerous—including mouse kidnapping—but ends well with them back at home, sharing a bowl of soup.

Why This Book Has Potential for Story Retelling

This is a story that can grow with children. Children love adventures, and enacting this story puts them in the cusp of danger. Another reason is that the setting and numerals end up the same: we end where we begin with the setting (inside the house), and we begin and end with "one." We start with one house and end with one soup, but Ruzzier still makes the circle, and we are left very satisfied at the end of this perfect little book.

Vocabulary

- rower
- nest
- ducklings
- shipwreck
- island
- beaks
- escape
- path
- cheers
- onions

Number Sense Concepts Addressed in the Story

- Sets of one, two, and three are repeated.
- A subtle pattern exists as the book unfolds: 123-321-123-321.

(continued on next page)

(continued from previous page)

Props/Visual Aids for Story Retelling

- Two mouse headbands of construction paper (see picture). The face of the mouse rests on top of the head above the eyes.
- If additional props are desired, see the book for ideas and use what is present in the classroom (such as carrots from the house center, rocks from outdoors, or a toy boat).
- Create two circles cut out of durable paper, or buy two pizza rounds or cake rounds.
- Find one large paper fastener to join the two circles together in the middle.

Directions

- Make or have children make the mouse headbands.
- Create a circle story frame to match the events in the story. Start by dividing one large circle into eight equal pie sections.
- The pattern of 123-321 repeats four times in the book, so write *1-2-3* in the first eighth. In the next section, write *3-2-1*. Repeat, clockwise, around the perimeter of the wheel.
- Add rough sketches near the appropriate numerals to offer a visual story-map structure for retelling.
- Cut out a $\frac{1}{8}$ sectional "pie" from the second circle.
- Place this second circle on top of the first, to cover everything on the wheel except one key section at a time. Fasten the two sections together.
- When retelling, children are better able to keep their places in the story if they use the story wheel as a prompt for what comes next. The wheel also serves as a focusing tool. Story retelling can proceed a step at a time with little reminders along the way. For older children, an arrow may suffice instead of hiding the rest of the story with a top cover.
- Use as few or as many props as you wish; children can pretend or enact the events as needed.
- See Recommended Resources for additional information.

Differentiation Strategies

- To simplify, expect fewer details and less mention of number in the early retellings. Consider coaching and narrating the story for children in the early stages of retelling, modeling how to use the circle story organizer using a talk-out-loud strategy while they enact the sequence as characters in the book.
- To provide a more challenging retelling experience, consider asking the child to enact or retell the story without the help of a narrator or the story organizer.

Additional Concepts

Adventures, cooking soup

Sparking Exploratory Play (What would happen if . . . ?)

- . . . the eaglets and ducklings followed the two mice home at the end? What would they do together?
- . . . the boat didn't sink but instead, kept traveling? Would there be a different adventure? What would happen?

Number Sense Concept: Counting Backward 10 to 1

Ten Little Fish by Audrey Wood and Bruce Wood (2004)

Ten plastic fish are all that are needed to retell this counting book.

Summary of the Story

This is a story of counting backward from ten to one, then increasing back to ten without counting.

Why This Book Has Potential for Story Retelling

The text is short, simple, and rhymes with most of the number words.

Vocabulary

- line
- crate
- heaven
- survive
- shore
- sea

Number Sense Concepts Addressed in the Story

- Counting down, ten to one
- Adding on

Props/Visual Aids for Story Retelling

- Ten plastic fish
- Blue felt or foam rectangle to serve as water

Directions

- Begin with a line of ten fish and enact the story, counting down and losing one fish at a time.

Differentiation Strategies

- To simplify the retelling, increase coaching. The fish are small but a safe size. Find larger fish if children have difficulty manipulating these small toys.
- To make the retelling more challenging, add numerals 1–10 to match to the sets of numbers as they emerge in the story. The book does not include numerals, only words.

Additional Concepts

Ocean life

Sparking Exploratory Play (What would happen if . . . ?)

- . . . all the fish became friends with the turtle? What would they play?

Number Sense Concepts: Counting to Seven

Counting Chickens by Polly Alakija (2014)

Children may retell the story in a simple framework by keeping track of the eggs and then the chicks, using seven finger-puppet chicks in plastic eggs as props.

Summary of the Story

A little boy in Africa waits for eggs to be laid, then waits for them to hatch, all while his friends' animals are born and growing.

Why This Book Has Potential for Story Retelling

Like *Two Mice*, this book offers several levels of retelling. First, young children may begin by retelling the basic story (with little to no math included). Another aspect of the story is that the friends' animals are also born in increasing increments. When children are ready for this level of retelling, add the other animals to the props. The story has multiple layers, and so I love the idea of revisiting the story over and over again with new levels of expectation and adding, when children are ready for it, a structure for retelling a complex story (the retelling calendar).

Vocabulary

- village
- cow, calf
- sheep, lambs
- goat, kids
- cat, kittens
- dog, puppies
- pig, piglets
- brood, hatch
- chicks, hen

Story Problems

- Everyone's animals were born and grew; Tobi's eggs just sat there for three weeks. The resolution is that after twenty-one days, the eggs hatched into chickens.

Number Sense Concepts Addressed in the Story

- Counting to seven
- Ordinal numbers

Props/Visual Aids for Story Retelling

- Straw hat
- 7 plastic eggs (may be opened and closed)
- 7 chick finger puppets
- Mother hen hand puppet (if desired)

Directions

- Place all chick finger puppets in the seven plastic eggs before retelling. Retell the story with children, and each time Mother Hen lays an egg, put one in the straw hat. Wait and wait and wait, and after twenty-one days, each chick will hatch.

(continued on next page)

(continued from previous page)

Differentiation Strategies

- To simplify, use only the plastic eggs, finger puppet chicks, and hat for retelling, and provide more scaffolding to the children.
- Make the retelling more complex by assigning each child a packet of animal puppets to use while enacting with teacher narration and prompting.
- Build toward complexity by adding a pocket chart or calendar, and gradually add retelling responsibilities to the group (see Recommended Resources for more information on retelling with calendars).
- Finally, to make story retelling the most challenging, move toward individual retellings.

Additional Concepts

Days of the week, waiting, chickens lay eggs and after twenty-one days they hatch and chicks are born

Sparking Exploratory Play (What would happen if ...?)

- ... each chick grew up to become a hen and laid eggs? (This question is posed on the last page of the book and makes for a great problem-solving task. Begin solving this problem by counting the original hen plus her seven grown chicks: eight hens. If eight hens lay seven eggs each, how many do we have? Act it out with either plastic eggs or manipulatives.)

Number Sense Concept: Part-Whole Relationships and Number Set Seven

Quack and Count by Keith Baker (1999)

Children enact part-to-whole concepts in this story by placing tongue-depressor ducklings in sets as described in the story.

Summary of the Story

This story is about a group of seven ducklings that explore the outdoors and in the process break into two parts to make a whole of seven. The vocabulary of addition is present in the book, but the author is not adding; instead, he describes each of the part-part-whole relationships of seven on each page. Near the end of the book, the ducks learn to fly.

Why This Book Has Potential for Story Retelling

The text is relatively simple and includes supportive rhymes to assist in the retelling. The set of seven is developmentally appropriate for fours and pre-Ks who are ready for exploring part-whole relationships.

Vocabulary

- row
- ducklings
- bumblebees
- shore
- leap
- dive
- paddling
- flapping

Number Sense Concepts Addressed in the Story

- Part-whole relationships

(continued on next page)

(continued from previous page)

Props/Visual Aids for Story Retelling

- Seven ducklings (any kind will work)
- If desired, create a wetland setting for the ducks to explore and split apart

Directions

- Enact the story with the seven ducks, starting in a row of seven, then moving systematically down by one through each possibility of part-part-whole relationships (for example, six and one ducklings, five and two ducklings, four and three ducklings, and so on).

Differentiation Strategies

- To simplify, scaffold the child in separating and regrouping the ducks; add a support structure, such as a storyboard, for retelling.
- To challenge children, consider adding numerals as labels to the parts and ask the child to read them.
- To extend the story, encourage breaking the seven ducks into more than two sets, such as sets of 3, 3, and 1 or 2, 2, 2, and 1 to represent the 7, for example.
- To further extend the story, consider taking away or adding ducklings to explore other number sets as part-part-whole relationships (for example, make the story into a set of ten ducklings and explore part-to-whole with those). Ask children to make up their own duck stories to go with them.

Additional Concepts

The vocabulary of addition, ducks, and wetlands environments

Sparking Exploratory Play (What would happen if . . . ?)

- . . . the ducks didn't fly away at the end?

Documenting and Assessing Young Children's Learning

Teachers are inquirers into children's learning and development. We document when children are making discoveries or building magnificent structures with blocks. We strive to understand their development in number sense, their understandings of shapes in our world, and whether they can use positional words in space while describing an airplane noticed during outdoor playtime. Teachers analyze whether children are developing in self-control, social skills, and their ability to take advice from adults. We identify their development of phonological awareness skills and observe alphabetic knowledge in young children as they hear the sounds in words and tell us the letters they notice in the environment or printed materials. Assessment strategies help us identify children's strengths and next areas in development which, of course, affects our teaching decisions.

In story retelling with young children, we want to know whether children enjoy the story, have fun with it, and play with word meanings and characters and story events along the way. In the process, we seek to understand where children are in a massive conglomeration of skills. Story retelling encompasses concepts of language development, oral language complexity, and narrative text. It involves organizational skills, summarizing skills, and connecting with the audience. We want to know what children are comprehending when they listen to and retell stories. We aspire to understand their conceptions of story structures. We look for ways to identify whether children are developing conceptual understanding of big ideas. We help them learn and identify elements of story by asking questions and drawing attention to characters, settings, plot, climax, and themes well before they learn to put labels to them later. We document their process skills in learning to tell and enact stories. Are children interacting with others, or are they isolative in the retelling process? Are they participative or collaborative when they choose retelling centers?

Teachers can observe retelling as it occurs, as shown in this picture, or they may choose to video- or audiotape the retelling for observation and analysis later.

Teachers compose plans, create environments, ask questions, implement strategies, conduct interventions, and differentiate instruction. And in the midst of our work with children, we investigate and analyze learning. We investigate children's learning in story retelling by documenting; like scientists, we collect data. In this regard, teachers are researchers of children's learning and our own teaching and program effectiveness. Teachers analyze by asking questions of the data that subsequently prompt changes or redirections in teaching.

One way teachers assess group learning and ask questions of our own teaching is by creating documentation or display panels, presenting the story-retelling experience to a wider audience of parents, the community, and others who attend the school. By including photographs of the experience, children's quotes, and a narrative providing the viewer with context or more academic benefits of the project that aren't typically visible, the viewer understands what is happening in the classroom and why. Inspired by Reggio Emilia educators, documentation and display panels are a way to communicate the story of learning to others (Filippinni and Vecchi 1996). They also serve as a way to analyze group learning experiences and offer a tool for reflection for both children and teachers. Table 8.1 describes how teachers may use the panel to share children's explorations and learning about stories and retelling with others.

Table 8.1 Example of One Format for Documentation-Display Panels on Story Retelling

Title of the Story Author / Illustrator		
Beginning (At first . . .)	**Middle (Then . . .)**	**Ending (Finally . . .)**
In the beginning of our story-retelling project, we read the story for enjoyment, then re-read it several times, paying special attention to word meanings and the problem at the heart of the story.	Next, our teacher modeled how to retell the story using props.	We told the story to each other.
	Insert picture of teacher retelling with props with a quote from what he is saying at the time.	*Insert pictures and related quotes.*
Insert photos of children listening to stories.	We learned how to retell the story with props in small groups.	*Capture several key story sections (as quotes) in children's words and post on this section of the board.*
	Insert photos of children in the midst of retelling with related quotes from children underneath.	
Insert quotes of children as they discuss meanings and problems in the story.	We told our own stories while playing with props.	*Include photos of the audience (children, parents, or other classes as relevant).*
	Insert related photos.	

When creating the panel, it is helpful to make sure the viewer is able to follow the sequence of the project timeline, thus "beginning," "middle," and "end" sections with borders. If you have poster-printing capabilities in the work environment or can afford to have a poster professionally printed, making the panels electronically affords a professional appearance. A cut-and-paste panel is just as magical because parents gather around photos of their children either way. In the case of Table 8.1 format for a panel, the title is placed at the top with a note about context or why we are doing the story-retelling project. The progression of the story is from left to right, but top-to-bottom progression is also easy for the viewer to follow. The big idea is to intentionally arrange the photos and quotes—to create a story. It's a way for you to retell the story of learning in your classroom.

The format above is a suggestion offered to help teachers get started on the journey of joyful documenting and communicating the story of learning. There are many ways to create documentation or display panels. Some are composed on 8½" x 11" paper with one photo and quotes highlighting the day, posted during naptime for parents to see at pickup time later that day and at drop-off time the next morning. Others are quite elaborate and emerge over time with collaborative work among teachers.

Documentation or display panels offer teachers a visual way to reflect on teaching and learning. Adjustments in teaching ultimately direct children's development in story retelling toward more accuracy and clarity while honoring children's need for playful learning. We want to know what worked in our teaching, what didn't work, and what we might do differently next time. We ask questions of the data to find out if children are indeed enjoying and appreciating stories, concept books, informational texts, and so on. We also want to know if children understand, develop, and participate in story-retelling activities. Before delving very deeply into assessing young children's development as story retellers, we consider ways to assess young children and review concerns regarding assessing young children.

Assessing Young Children

Because of the nature of young children and the paths of developing story-retelling skills, teachers are offered rich assessment opportunities in their day-to-day work. Assessing while children are engaged in play, interacting, learning, and doing what they typically do during the school day is considered *authentic assessment*. There is nothing contrived about the assessment—teachers observe and document by collecting children's drawings and other work samples, filling out a checklist, taking notes, or filling out a form while children are involved in their work or play or interaction with each other. Collecting data from children could include taking photographs of children retelling with a partner or creating structures during centers time. Teachers could photocopy children's illustrations, and children can cut out and glue the copies to a tongue depressor to become a puppet in a story, or capture interaction as small groups of children plan to take on different roles. Capturing children enacting or retelling a story on video or audio recordings allows teachers to revisit data for careful assessment and analysis later.

When teachers use data to inform their next steps in teaching, they are collecting data as a formative assessment. Formative assessment strategies inform teachers of where children are in the learning process and may be either authentic as described in the previous paragraph or conducted outside of the learning experience. Most of the time, formative assessments in preschool are observational—we observe children while they are engaged in learning or interacting—and we do this because we prefer not to interrupt children while they are engaged. Alternatively, sometimes preschool and kindergarten teachers interrupt themselves while they are reading either to ask a question or to clarify what children are thinking (or they'll ask for a thumbs up if children understand the concept or a thumbs down if they don't). The teacher is stopping the activity of listening to the story and conducting a quick formative assessment that disengages children from the direct teaching experience. Inquiring into what children know and do while they are interacting and participating in story retelling helps teachers understand what young children are learning and where we need to make teaching adjustments to ensure they can progress in development and understanding.

When we reach the end of a story-retelling project, we may wish to document how far children progressed during the experience or where they are in the story-retelling continuum. This is known as a *summative assessment*. Authentic summative assessments are natural for story retelling because we typically end the project with a performance for a friend, a group, our classroom, or other guests. Videotaping the final performance is almost expected in our media-saturated culture. Using the video coupled with teacher analysis as a summative assessment is useful particularly with electronic portfolio systems.

Cautions in Assessing Young Children

The same assessment issues inherent in our work in early childhood education also complicate the assessment of story retelling. First, children's interest levels may be with story retelling one day but not the day one assesses. This is why authentic assessment is the most powerful—we assess when we can document what children are doing. Second, young children's attention spans, though noted as lengthy when engaged in project-oriented work, may not be amenable to assessing from time to time. Third, assessment forms may be limiting and might not demonstrate what children can do but instead provide an overall look at what they cannot do. Fourth, assessing in preschool classrooms is challenging due to the number of children we are assessing, their ability levels, and all the existing assessment demands in our assessment-frenzied educational culture. Finally, there is no one right way to assess all children ages three to five in story retelling, and the same goes for kindergarteners. Children come to school with different skills and concepts; there is no one form or assessment strategy that can answer to all children's developmental needs at the same time. Therefore I offer varied ways to assess story retelling later in this chapter as a way of supporting teachers in their data collection and documentation efforts and sparking their own endeavors in creating assessment tools to serve their young students' learning needs.

In addition to issues in assessing young children in general, story retelling offers its own assessment issues. First, not all stories are created equally. Literature for the young child is varied in complexity and in genre. In early childhood, concept books abound. Literature for the young child also includes stories that we sing or fingerplay, familiar stories that children hear at home, and stories they have not heard before. It represents nonfiction as well as additional genres. Our work in story retelling includes trying to expose children to samples of a wide variety of literature representative of diverse families, ethnicities, socioeconomic levels, and cultures. Stories with problems (or goals) that lead to an eventual climax and resolution (or attainment of the goal) are especially important for retelling. Although children's literature is rife with stories without any problems or goals, McGee and Schickedanz indicate that stories with problems are more difficult for young children to discern yet crucial to their literacy development (2007). We are compelled to include more sophisticated stories for our young learners.

So which stories do we assess? To further complicate this puzzle, at which level of involvement do we expect preschool and kindergarten children to be retelling? How do we assess a child's retelling of just three words? A child might retell with a friend—is this okay for assessing? Shouldn't a child retell alone if we are really assessing? Or what about enacting—where children participate in a group to retell a story and take on role playing? No wonder assessing story retelling is such an inexact science.

Frequent assessment of young children while they are engaged in authentic activities offers us the highest-quality data, rather than assessing once every quarter in contrived scenarios. Assessment complications include that children's interest levels may wane on the day a teacher plans to assess story retelling: the story selection may not appeal to the child, the vocabulary could be unfamiliar to the child, the child might not relate to the illustrations or props, the child wishes to do something else, and so on. In addition, children may not take teachers very seriously when asked to retell a story (for assessment purposes). I can just imagine a child thinking "This teacher read and worked with us on this story in small groups—she surely knows the story by now! Why do I need to retell it to her when I can be playing with Maggie in the blocks center?"

Practicing teachers may find it frustrating to assess children in story retelling with a one-size-fits-all assessment: children have varied abilities and interests and attention spans. Following are assessment strategies that address several story-retelling emphasis areas.

Assessing Story Retelling

Indicators of story retelling with young children fall in multiple areas, more so than in the primary grades. First-, second-, and third-grade teachers focus only on children's inclusion of elements of story while retelling the story for others. More frequently (and regretfully), story retelling in primary grades has evolved into writing and filling out worksheets (which were originally created for organizing oral retelling) rather than telling. Even though writing is quite a legitimate way to spin a yarn, I fear our accountability and efficiency emphasis in teaching has taken the telling out of story retelling in the primary grades.

In preschool and kindergarten, indicators of story retelling include more than just the story itself. Indicators of communication and oral language are always developing and worthy of early childhood assessment attention. Because indicators of play and creativity are so valued and crucial to learning in preschool and kindergarten, assessment of these areas partly monitors the joy factor we are striving to achieve in retelling. Although we are, like our primary-grade counterparts, working toward accuracy in literature-based story retelling, we still honor children's need for being creative with stories—which is why it is necessary to include creative retelling as an indicator in assessment. Teachers encourage creativity among our young students, and it is, in fact, part of the nature of childhood, so we document it and learn what it reveals about the child, story, and process of moving toward accuracy. In primary grades, children earn points for accuracy; in preschool and kindergarten, the weight of story-retelling assessments fall on the teacher.

With English-language learners and children who have exceptionalities in language development, we assess and document expressive language as it occurs in story retelling. We also consider ways to scaffold and support children and describe what they can do with assistance. How are children manipulating props or responding to our prompts? A story-retelling experience for some children may focus on naming and labeling props or visual aids along with the retelling and enacting; we begin with what children know and can relate, and work from there.

Finally, understanding indicators of story structures, elements, and comprehension are of keen interest to the preschool and kindergarten teacher. Although communicating meaning, developing language, promoting joy, and honoring creativity are part of assessing young children, tracking children's development as they include elements of story is indeed at the heart of story retelling. In the following sections, I define indicators of story retelling. Assessments in this chapter are designed to be used in the classroom but are also intended to spark or challenge teachers into designing assessments more relevant to their own situations.

Observations of Play and Creativity in Story Retelling

Teachers of young children recognize creativity and playfulness in children's language and retelling. We encourage children to play with story because we want them to apply the vocabulary of story with each other so they can both associate words with experiences in similar categories and seal the meanings in their minds for future use. The key indicators of playful and creative story retelling are noted when children make up new stories, add characters, or make changes to the story in any way. Playing with story is a valid way for young children to apply learning, as well as to learn from each other. "Catching" children at play with stories and props, then sharing the event with others through documentation-displays or portfolios is one way to communicate children's creative processes and learning through play with others.

It should be noted that children sometimes focus on the visual meaning projected in the illustrations, which may differ from the narrative. Addressing the illustrations while interacting over stories during read-alouds can bring illustrations into light and will help teachers understand whether children's story ideas are contrived or have a source in the book.

Often children will try out words they don't typically use, and in fact, the use of Tier Two words—sophisticated words—may show up in play in more formal settings, such as small-group work. Watching for children to apply story-related vocabulary words in the context of play is authentic to the child and offers us documentation that children are indeed learning and applying Tier Two words.

Form 8.1 provides teachers a basic observation form focused on literature-based play experiences that provide insight into children's interests and processes in learning story retelling. (Note that full-size versions of all forms in this chapter appear in the back of the book.) When observing children in literature-based play episodes, look for the following indicators and document observations:

- Uses story-related vocabulary

- Enacts story-related plot events

- Adds creative innovations on the story, such as changing or adding new story plot events, new characters, or changes in characters' behavior, props, or setting

- Creates new stories with story props representing characters

- Includes characters or events in their own play scenarios

Form 8.1 Observation of Story Retelling in Free Play

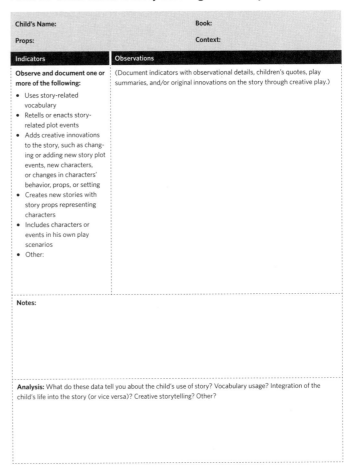

| Child's Name: | Book: |
| Props: | Context: |

Indicators	Observations
Observe and document one or more of the following: • Uses story-related vocabulary • Retells or enacts story-related plot events • Adds creative innovations to the story, such as changing or adding new story plot events, new characters, or changes in characters' behavior, props, or setting • Creates new stories with story props representing characters • Includes characters or events in his own play scenarios • Other:	(Document indicators with observational details, children's quotes, play summaries, and/or original innovations on the story through creative play.)

Notes:

Analysis: What do these data tell you about the child's use of story? Vocabulary usage? Integration of the child's life into the story (or vice versa)? Creative storytelling? Other?

(Note: Form 8.2 may also be used to document play-based story retelling if several children are playing at once.)

Documenting Children's Participation in Story Retelling through the Dramatic Arts

Teachers offer familiar stories for early retelling experiences, but that doesn't mean we can't or shouldn't play with more complex narratives. Complex stories offer children opportunities to grow in vocabulary and experience story structure first hand. When teachers use supportive approaches, complex stories can be quite motivating. Acting out stories with teachers directing and supporting children's participation leads toward overall success. Helping children to be successful in early story-retelling experiences supports our goal of creating lovers of literature and language in playful ways.

Chen and McNamee serve as a key reference for those teachers who are sincerely interested in documenting and assessing enactments in their classrooms (2007). Their bridging method takes authentic assessment into great depth and detail in providing levels of development in story acting for analysis along with several additional assessment strategies. Briefly, Chen and McNamee include one assessment with multiple indicators related to "participation, body movement, vocal/facial expression, and social awareness" when acting (130). Second and third assessments evaluate and describe children's "working approach" toward acting out a story (131–32), while a fourth assessment offers a "performance rubric" for acting (133). Chen and McNamee are known for their work in linking analysis back to teacher practice and planning, and they do so with story acting.

One way to document role playing as it occurs is to use an open-ended observation form based on one created by Pamela Oken-Wright to document interaction (personal conversation, February 26, 1999). When observing children in a group setting, Oken-Wright was able to document conversations as they occurred in real time by writing in what one child would say as well as responses from other children in the group, moving down the form as time and conversations progressed. As children changed in the group, she would pull another form and continue on with the documentation. Using her format and applying it to story enacting, teachers may document key conversations, use of story-related vocabulary, and what children say about the story in their own words. Form 8.2 offers teachers one way to document children's story enactments through role playing. It may be especially useful to videotape a practice or

Form 8.2 Documenting Story Retelling through Acting: Group Enactment Form (adapted with permission from Pamela Oken-Wright)

Book:				Date & Time:
Context:				
Child's Name Role Played	Child's Name Role Played	Child's Name Role Played	Child's Name Role Played	Teacher Reflections

Notes about taking direction, participation, expression, social awareness, enjoyment, playfulness/creativity, accuracy in meaning of lines, and use of props (if applicable):

performance, show the performance to the group, then ask for their thoughts about their performances. Videotaping offers a way for teachers to capture key data and use the observation form in selective episodes (for example, capturing the use of story-related vocabulary or a particularly insightful line created by a child that demonstrates understanding of key concepts). The form may also be used in a free-play scenario where children likely take more creative license with their roles.

Participative Story Retelling and Fingerplays

When we consider fingerplays, rhymes, songs, and participative stories as early retelling experiences, assessing their indicators is an educational step toward building skills for successful story retelling. Participative story retelling is typically learned and performed as a group. Perhaps this is why it is a good place to begin building skills for retelling: group participation offers a nonthreatening learning environment. Participation, therefore, as part of the learning process in interactive stories, is a key indicator to assess. Also part of the learning process is how children approach the task, including their dispositions or demeanors. What is the child's emotional state? Has the child participated with the group? Does the child understand and apply the appropriate responses or interactions or fingerplay actions? The indicator *learning process* includes both participation and approach/demeanor.

In addition to assessing learning process, we may look for whether children know the words and, if applicable, the tunes that go with the fingerplay, song, rhyme, or group interactive story. Do children know the actions that go with their stories? Do they use props appropriately? Do children need prompts when they retell or sing or provide interaction in a group story experience? Assessing these indicators offers insight into early retelling skills in group settings. Over time assessment provides a glimpse into how children respond to a task in group experiences.

Assessing serves as a tool for looking at our own practice. As we document and assess children's growth, we also reflect on practice. Are we offering varied interactive retelling experiences to children? Are they getting a wide range of songs, fingerplays, and rhymes to build literacy skills? Are children provided opportunities to participate

Form 8.3 **Class Checklist: Fingerplays, Rhymes, Songs, and Participative Story Retelling**

Book:					Date:
Children's Names	Learning Process: *Participates; Shows Enjoyment and Interest*	Knows Words and Tunes	Includes Actions or Uses Props or Visual Aids	Teacher Prompt Needed	Observations What stands out in child's learning process? Knowledge of words and tunes? Actions or props?

Comprehension & Vocabulary Questions:

with actions, sound effects, and repeated phrases when a story is read aloud? Form 8.3 relies on the aforementioned indicators to form a quick checklist for teachers.

Assessing Children's Retellings of Concept Books

When assessing the retelling of a concept book, the biggest priority is determining if the child is getting the concept right (accuracy in sequence or other elements in the book, for example). Bill Martin Jr. addressed the concept of color in *Brown Bear, Brown Bear*. Teachers organize the retelling of *Brown Bear* for children who are in the early phases of retelling by using the endpapers of the book as a guide to the sequence of the story. Creating a strip of colors out of construction paper that provides a key to the sequence for children can offer an opportunity for successful retelling. This way, teachers can check conceptual understanding of what the story is addressing: color. When children say, "Brown Bear, Brown Bear . . . ," do they pick up the appropriate prop (the brown one)? If looking for the red bird, will they select the correct prop? Later teachers can add an indicator for sequence in the checklist for the more experienced child. When teachers remove the strip of construction paper colors that served as the key to the sequence for children, children are required to organize the sequence themselves. How will they remember the sequence for accurate retelling? Are they aware there is a sequence? Does it matter to the child if the sequence gets off, or does the child not appear to mind? Form 8.4 provides an example for how teachers may choose to assess concept book retellings.

Form 8.4 Checklist for Retelling a Concept Book

Book:					
Concept Addressed:					
List Children's Names	Enjoys / Holds Interest in Retelling	Accurate Use of Concept	Accurate Use of Props or Visual Aids	Teacher Prompt Needed	Observations & Notes

Comprehension & Vocabulary Questions:

Notes on How the Child Sequences the Retelling:

Discovering Children's Favorite and Familiar Stories

The best way to learn about children's story experiences is to ask their families. Having several methods of acquiring this information increases the chances of being successful: interview parents during an initial home visit; send home a survey with the child or mail it to the child's home; and/or e-mail a link to an online survey to collect information. Here are some questions relevant to children's home reading background that may provide a starting point for teachers in creating their own surveys or questionnaires:

- Do you or another family member read to your child at home? How often?
- Do you ever tell stories to your child at home? How often?
- Does your child have favorite stories? If so, please list the titles below.
- Would you be willing to audiotape a story in your child's home language for your child to listen to at our center or school?

Teachers urge families to read at home with children and may host family reading celebrations and events at school to promote the joy and benefits of reading with young children.

Once we have discovered favorite stories and created prop boxes for them, we must determine how to assess children in an open-ended way. We do so in a manner that honors what children can do with assistance rather than what they cannot do alone. One unified message across much of the literature on story retelling with very young children is a message of supporting young children's early literacy experiences so they are positive. Researchers and authors of story-retelling literature agree that story retelling with young children should always be positive, playful, and supportive. Just as using props and visual aids is highly recommended, so, too, is supporting children with prompts when needed. Thus, any assessment conducted on behalf of young children should demonstrate that teacher prompts and support are an expectation in the assessment process. Prompting supports children to move beyond what they can do alone (Bodrova and Leong 2006). It is an effective and efficient way to teach, because this is teaching in the zone—the zone of proximal development (Vygotsky 1978).

Assessing Children as They Retell Fictional Stories

In chapter 2, indicators of story structures, elements, and teaching for vocabulary building and comprehension were identified and addressed. Those elements serve as a starting point for developing more detailed assessments of narrative story retellings.

Assessments that analyze young children's development of narrative retelling of literature-based stories typically include key elements in story, plot episodes, theme, resolutions, and sequence (Morrow 2015; Morrow, Roskos, and Gambrell 2015). The practice of assessing young children in narrative story retelling assumes that children have experience listening to a story repeatedly, participating in interactive read-aloud discussions with the group, and understanding vocabulary and overall meaning of the story. It assumes that teachers have modeled story retelling to children and that children have subsequently participated in guided play and/or other learning experiences in enacting or retelling with props or visual aids. Children need ample experiences with playing and practicing and developing as story retellers.

Prompting is a way of assisting children. Young children are developing working memory, an executive functioning skill. Collaborative story retelling may be a good strategy while teaching and assessing in these cases. Collaborative retelling progresses the story and allows teachers to check in with children on their understanding of parts of the story. In this case, children and teachers may retell different parts of the story together—or teachers may tell a large part of the story, then pause for children to fill in. Indicate in the notes section if collaborative retelling is used in the assessment. We provide prompts when children need help; retelling with teacher prompts demonstrates what children can do with assistance. In early childhood classrooms, knowing what children can do with assistance helps us teach children effectively because we are supporting children in their next steps in development.

For preschoolers new to story retelling, English-language learners, and children with language exceptionalities, descriptors of narrative story may be overwhelming and inappropriate as a meaningful assessment strategy. In developing a more general view of narrative retelling—an assessment with fewer details and, instead, a quick view of child performance as a whole—we can look at the literature on how children develop their own creative stories, as dictated to their teachers, for example. Research by Applebee (1978) on how children conceptualized stories from the early childhood years through age seventeen identified developmental patterns of narrative storytelling. Chen and McNamee (2007) adapted Applebee's work with children age three to third grade and applied it to assessing stories (both creative and literature-based) that were dictated by children to their teachers. Chen and McNamee's assessment tool includes eleven different levels in which children's story retelling could be identified. Significant is that Morrow's research (1986) with kindergarten children demonstrated that literature-based story retelling had a positive impact on children's dictated stories. Form 8.5 reflects a further modification of Applebee's work and Chen and McNamee's levels of story dictation. Note that Chen and McNamee offer eleven levels of story dictation, and I've truncated them down to six more-generalized levels applicable to preschool and early kindergarten in form 8.5.

Form 8.5 Story Retelling: Levels and Observations (adapted from children's development in creative story dictation (Chen and McNamee 2007 with permission from Corwin.)

Select One	Indicators	Check (✔) If Prompted	Child Observations or Teacher Notes
Refusal	Refuses to retell story or speak (no word utterances).		
1–3 words	Speaks one to three words that are not connected to each other but may be relevant to the story.		
Sentence or list	Retells the story in either a sentence or list with little to no plot or action or characterization.		
Undeveloped ideas	Retells a number of undeveloped events, thoughts, concepts, or characters related to the story but lacks the essence, key ideas, central idea, or characters behind a story.		
String of ideas	Retells by stringing together ideas as if telling a story without a central theme or idea; lacks plot, continuity, central characters, and focus.		
Central idea but not fully developed	Retells with a central theme or character or concept but lacks continuity and is not fully developed.		
Main idea prevails	The story includes elements and characters central to the plot where the main idea of the story prevails. The central plot is revealed as a problem or goal.		
Generally accurate	Story retelling is overall accurate. It includes many of the essentials: beginning, middle, and end; problem and solution (or goal and how goal was met); characters; setting (time and place); plot sequence and overall theme; and details.		

Name: _____ Date: _____

Book: _____

Most existing assessments of story retelling designed for young children (Morrow 2015; Morrow, Roskos, and Gambrell 2016) address inclusion of key story descriptors. Typically we see a provision for assessing elements of story by using three methods: (1) numeric or quantitative assessment—offering a score for each component included in the retelling; (2) collection of child utterances or qualitative assessment—providing observational notes on key wording used in the retelling; or (3) a checklist—where teachers check off when a certain element or plot event, for example, is included. These retelling assessment tools are user-friendly and helpful to teachers.

Form 8.5 is designed to offer a more detailed assessment of story retelling by including those components of story we expect to hear when we listen to someone tell a story. The checklist that follows should not be interpreted as a list of expectations for proficient retelling among all preschool or kindergarten children. Instead, the purpose of the observation form is to provide a list of indicators that may appear while teachers support story-retelling episodes with young children. It is designed to serve as a guide for understanding where children are developmentally as they retell a story.

In form 8.5, a more detailed listing of indicators of narrative text is included. Like form 8.5, a column is included for noting teacher prompts. I recommend recording children's story retelling not only for the sake of accuracy and sharing with families, but also to document key words or interesting sentences. Highlights can be drawn from the recordings to demonstrate growth, changes, and vocabulary use. Form 8.6 is a combined checklist with room for writing the child's words and teacher notes.

The nature of authentic assessment suggests that formative assessment strategies occur while children are engaged in story-retelling experiences. Summative assessment is conducted at the end (as a last retelling or enactment) or culmination of a story-retelling project. This form is designed to meet both formative and summative assessment needs and may accompany children's recordings and serve as a more formalized assessment component in electronic portfolios.

Table 8.2 offers an example of how the teacher fills out the form prior to collecting data.

Form 8.6 Literature-Based Story-Retelling Checklist and Observations

Name:			Date:	
Book:				
Context:				
Indicators	**Check (✔) If Prompted**	**Story's Descriptors**	**Child's Descriptors Used While Retelling the Story**	**Check (✔) If Prompted**
Characters				
Setting				
Repeated Lines/Key Vocabulary				
Plot Sequence/ Events/Organization				
Problem or Goal				
Resolution or How Goal Was Met				
Comprehension Questions:				
Inference Questions:				
Notes:				

Table 8.2: Example of the Literature-Based Story-Retelling Checklist and Observations
(This example demonstrates the teacher's preparation before child's retelling episode.)

Child's Name: Denzell Lewis   **Date:** January 17, 2018

Title: *Goldilocks and the Three Bears*

Context: The story is a familiar one for Denzell. We read the story every day last week with different topics of focus (in whole group the first day and small group thereafter). After I modeled the retelling this week, Denzell participated in group retelling experiences during small-group time on three occasions. Denzell played with the bears and Goldilocks in the house center on 1/15 with two friends for 20 minutes.

Indicators	Check (✔) If Present	Story's Descriptors	Child's Descriptors Used While Retelling the Story	Check (✔) If Prompted
Characters		4 characters: • Mama Bear • Papa Bear • Baby Bear • Goldilocks		
Setting		• Woods (outdoors) • House (in the woods) • Kitchen • Family room • Bedroom		
Repeated Lines/Key Vocabulary		• "It was toooo…" (hot or cold or soft or hard) • "It was juuust right."		
Plot Sequence/ Events/ Organization		5 key plot events: • Porridge was too hot, so the Bear family went for a walk. • Goldilocks tasted all the porridge, then ate all Baby Bear's porridge. • Goldilocks sat in all the chairs, then broke Baby Bear's chair. • Goldilocks lay in all the beds before sleeping in Baby Bear's bed. • Goldilocks woke up and ran out of the house.		

(continued on next page)

(continued from previous page)

Indicators	Check (✔) If Present	Story's Descriptors	Child's Descriptors Used While Retelling the Story	Check (✔) If Prompted
Problem or Goal		The Bear family came back and found eaten porridge, destroyed chairs, and Goldilocks asleep in Baby Bear's bed.		
Resolution or How Goal was Met		Goldilocks awoke and fled the Bears' home.		

Comprehension Questions:

- Why did the three bears leave their home?
- Why did they come home?
- What was the problem in the story?

Check with Denzell about the meaning of "porridge."

Inference Questions:

- How do you think the Bear family felt when they discovered Goldilocks in Baby Bear's bed?
- Why do you think Goldilocks entered the house even though the bears were not at home?

Notes:

Indicators of Communication and Oral Language

Communication skills are crucial in everything we do. Children especially must be able to communicate their needs and listen to adults when advice or direction is provided. Communication skills are critical to social and emotional development in young children, but assessing them can be a complex task. Primary components of oral language include word choice, expression, organization, content, and description.

Oral language complexity may be captured while children retell when they label feelings ("sad"), which is a higher level than using descriptors ("cried"). Children may choose to include both the label and descriptor ("Tommy cried. He was sad."). Yet another indicator of language complexity is found in using words such as *because* to tell why: "Tommy cried because he was sad." Oral language complexity is also noted when children communicate sequence to their audiences by using higher levels of communication and use transition words to help the audience follow the story: *then* or *before* or *first*.

Although we are less concerned with grammar tense accuracy in preschool and kindergarten, all children are developing language in pre-K and kindergarten, and we ask whether young students are interpreting the story information accurately in the retellings. Story vocabulary and content may be such that the child is misinterpreting the story in the retelling. Are young children able to structure and organize language for retelling, demonstrating language complexity? Are they learning to communicate over time by adding accurate sequence to the characters and increasingly adding helpful transitions for the audience? Our work with English-language learners in preschool and kindergarten compels us to adjust to the level of the child and document nonverbal (receptive) understanding, such as pointing to props and expressive language as they develop and grow in our classrooms.

Although they precede writing, oral language and story retelling support language and literacy development. Riley and Burrell noted that the New Zealand Story Retelling Task (part of their school entrance assessment at the time) focused strongly on oral communication skills in assessing story retelling in young children (2007). Their research, spanning the first two years of school, substantiated previous studies, which demonstrates validity and reliability in the New Zealand Story Retelling Task. The assessment addressed sentence structure, vocabulary, organization, description and expression, and content (2007, 184–85). The New Zealand task additionally delved into comprehension and inference by including questions to the child pertaining to the text at the end of the assessment. Similarly, Spencer, Kajian, Petersen, and Bilyk (2014) used the Narrative Language Measures, which measure children's story structure and language complexity. They used story-retelling tasks as interventions with preschool children with developmental disabilities, then measured impact—the results of which were positive. Neither of these assessments are literature based or focused on authentic learning experiences (one was an intervention, the other a school readiness assessment), but their work informs teachers of the relevance of retelling as a venue for monitoring oral language and communication and the power of assessment in understanding children's learning in story retelling.

When assessing oral language and communication in story retelling in pre-K and kindergarten, teachers look for the following indicators: word choices, expression, organization, content, descriptions, and other indicators that may be unique to the child or situation or story (Riley and Burrell 2007). Definitions follow:

- **Word choices, vocabulary, and sentence structure.** This indicator refers to use of wording while retelling that captures the author's voice and notes particular wording in the story. Teachers look for appropriate applications of story-related vocabulary and words that help describe characters, places, or time in the story as relevant, for example. They document how children communicate sentences.

- **Expression.** In retelling, this refers to intonation in the voice but also includes facial expressions.

- **Organization.** This indicator pertains to how the child meets organizational structures built within the story—including an introduction in the beginning, offering a clear middle, and providing an ending. More-advanced story retellers will start offering transitions, such as "Once upon a time," or including some of the indicators of oral language complexity by saying "First" or using words that demonstrate cause and effect, such as *because* or *so*. Children communicate sequence by ordering it, and this often falls under organization and oral language complexity. Yet with young children and early retellers, props and teacher-created organizational structures often serve as reminders of sequence. We are focused on how the child uses language to organize the story and sequence (as an oral communication indicator).

- **Content**. In story retelling, this pertains to what happens in the story or what the story (or information or concept) is about in an accurate manner.

- **Descriptions**. In story retelling, the child provides essential information about characters or plot events. The child may provide extra, superfluous information as well. Questions one may ask about description are: Does the child include descriptive details unique to this version of the story? Make up details? Include details that appear in the illustrations yet are not in the text?

- **Other**. in noting nuances or language unique to the child, teachers note significant developments in the child's retelling progression, particularly in oral language complexity as the child becomes more experienced in retelling.

Form 8.7 is designed as an observational tool for documenting indicators of communication and oral language demonstrated by an individual child while retelling. The observational form may be used either as a formative assessment while children are developing story-retelling skills in small-group work or as a summative assessment at the culmination of the story-retelling project. The tool holds potential to inform teachers of children's strengths and next steps in development with regard to oral language use and communication.

Form 8.7 Observations of Communication and Oral Language Displayed in Story Retelling (adapted from the terminology used in the New Zealand School Entry Assessment Story Retelling Task, as reported by Riley and Burrell 2007, with permission from the New Zealand Ministry of Education)

Name:		Date:
Book:		

Indicator	Observations
Word choices, vocabulary, and sentence structure	
Expression	
Organization	
Content	
Descriptions	
Other	
Comprehension Check:	
Notes:	

Afterword

Hearing the Voice of the Storyteller

Our work in story retelling is centered on helping young children develop and apply language and literacy skills and concepts across the curriculum. Skills and concepts developed in story retelling are foundational to comprehending text as children learn to read. Our work with children is also centered within joyful experiences while children believe they are truly playing when teachers set up small groups, allow for exploration, and take children toward learning objectives in the context of playful story retelling. The joy of telling a story is empowering to children, and it is made possible by teachers like you.

Ashley Bryan, author and illustrator of more than fifty children's books, many of which are award winners, writes about his life in *Ashley Bryan: Words to My Life's Song* (2009). Among his many awards and honors, Bryan won the prestigious Laura Ingalls Wilder Award in 2009. Near the closing of the book, he writes about his editor, Jean Karl, who in 1962 posed a question that helped him move beyond the role of illustrating books and into the world of writing children's books as well.

> "So, Ashley, tell the stories in your own words," she told me.
>
> To get the spirit of the oral tradition for my writing, I practiced reading aloud from the Black American poets. . . . I then retold the African tales using the good ideas from poetry in my writing. I hoped this would open the ear to the sound of the voice in the printed word, so that even when reading my stories silently, readers would hear the voice of a storyteller. (49)

The voice of a storyteller. Hearing the voice of a storyteller. I'm thrust back into my childhood, invisible again so the story and the moment won't go away. Only this time, you are the voice of the storyteller. Your power as an educator reaches many children and families in your work. As you work with children in developing their own voices, I wish you joyful story retelling!

Recommended Resources

Collections of Fingerplays, Poems, and Songs for Young Children

Froebel, the father of the kindergarten, wrote a book about rhymes, games, fingerplays, and songs based on what German mothers were singing and playing with their children. Froebel's work was influenced by his mentor, Pestalozzi, who wrote a book based on Gertrude, his maid and nanny to his children: *How Gertrude Teaches Her Children.* Gertrude used little rhymes and songs as educational tools, and as far as we know, Pestalozzi was the first to document such things for educational purposes (Cole, [1950] 2007).

I am especially fond of the following two children's finger playbooks, because the author-illustrator, Marc Brown (of Arthur and D.W. fame), included illustrations of hand motions right alongside the words—a rare find these days!

- Brown, Marc. 1985. *Hand Rhymes: Collected and Illustrated by Marc Brown.* New York: Puffin Unicorn.

- ———. 2013. *Marc Brown's Playtime Rhymes: A Treasury for Families to Learn and Play Together.* New York: Little, Brown.

The following two children's books are collections of both songs and poems for children that include CDs to help with cadence in the poetry and tune with the songs.

- Beaton, Clare. 2008. *Playtime Rhymes for Little People.* Vocals by Susan Reed. Cambridge, MA: Barefoot Books.

- Van Hout, Mies. 2014. *Twinkle, Twinkle, Little Star.* Music by the Chambers Family. Lemniscaat, Rotterdam, The Netherlands.

Additional collections are as follows; both are high-quality literature:

- Ada, Alma Flor, F. Isabel Campoy, and Alice Schertle. 2003. *¡Pío Peep! Traditional Spanish Nursery Rhymes.* Illustrated by Viví Escrivá. New York: Rayo.

- Orozco, José-Luis. 2002. *Diez Deditos and Other Play Rhymes and Action Songs from Latin America.* Illustrated by Elisa Kleven. New York: Dutton Children's Books.

This poetry book is still a best seller and is a terrific resource for teachers and parents of young children.

- Prelutsky, Jack, ed. 1986. *Read-Aloud Rhymes for the Very Young.* Illustrated by Marc Brown. New York: Alfred A Knopf.

The following poetry anthology is one I purchased when I was teaching young children—it is billed as a top-selling poetry book today. I expect that its success as a good resource lies in its emphases on early childhood education themes: seasons, families, weather, bugs, and so on.

- Prelutsky, Jack, ed. 1983. *The Random House Book of Poetry for Children: A Treasury of 572 Poems for Today's Child.* Illustrated by Arnold Lobel. New York: Random House.

Naturally, an Internet search will help you find fingerplays, songs, and poems, but a great teacher resource book helps as well. Following are two teacher resources that are especially helpful:

- Cobb, Jane, ed. 1996. *I'm a Little Teapot! Presenting Preschool Storytime.* Illustrations by Magda Lazicka. Vancouver, BC: Black Sheep Press.

- Herr, Judy. 2013. *Creative Resources for the Early Childhood Classroom.* 6th ed. Belmont, CA: Wadsworth, Cengage Learning.

Resources on Story Retelling with Young Children

- Hoyt, Linda. 2009. *Revisit, Reflect, Retell: Time-Tested Strategies for Teaching Reading Comprehension.* Portsmouth, NH: Heinemann.

- Huff, Mary Jo. 2011. *Story Play: Building Language and Literacy One Story at a Time.* Silver Springs, MD: Gryphon House.

Songs: Selected Books for Story Retelling and Enacting

- Cabrera, Jane. 2003. *If You're Happy and You Know It!* New York: Scholastic.

- Cauley, Lorinda Bryan. 1992. *Clap Your Hands.* New York: Scholastic.

- Emberley, Rebecca, and Ed Emberley. 2013. *The Itsy Bitsy Spider.* Portsmouth, NH: Two Little Birds.

- Hoberman, Mary Ann. 2003. *Miss Mary Mack.* Illustrated by Nadine Bernard Wescott. New York: Little, Brown.

- Simpson, Steve. 2009. *The Farmer in the Dell.* New York: Scholastic.

- Taback, Simms. 1997. *There Was an Old Lady Who Swallowed a Fly.* New York: Viking.

Examples of Books and Graphic Organizers for Story Retelling

Graphic organizers provide order to information so we can understand it. Using words and pictures, graphic organizers have been demonstrated as useful tools when teaching young children.

Teachers in elementary schools use graphic organizers to teach children about the elements of story. With young children, elementary-level graphic organizers are meaningless. Instead, our graphic organizers follow the story in sequence. When I make graphic organizers for young children, my intention is to provide as much support as possible by simplifying the organizational structure of the story and adding pictures or icons to help children remember the sequence. The graphic organizer is a short or quick view of the story and should help (not confuse) children in the retelling. It offers the structure to children in an understandable way by supplying a visual or concrete reminder of how the story is organized: lines for add-on stories, zigzags for stories that might have happy-sad-happy patterns, or circles when books end where they begin. Graphic organizers for story retelling are often much more "physical" in nature—they allow us to walk through a path, hold a circle, or stack a story using built-in self-checking mechanisms.

When making graphic organizers, try not to glue down the visual aids to make them permanent (one exception is the "story in a pie" organizer listed in the circle-story table). Visual aids are pictures, icons, colors, or dots that we place on the graphic organizer while retelling. Instead of making these reminders permanent on the graphic organizer, use Velcro to attach them. In early retellings, the child receives the graphic organizer with all the pictures in place (set up by you), and either the child points to the pictures as he retells or he has a bag of props to use—and follows the sequence and pictures on the graphic organizer. This graphic organizer is a heavily supportive visual aid for retelling. Alternatively, the graphic organizer used with all the pictures set aside requires the child to supply the props or visual aids in sequence—a more challenging way to retell. Imagine a child using only colors (the key) and no props to retell *Brown Bear, Brown Bear*; some children in preschool classrooms are ready for this. Try to support children by including the following consistently across your graphic organizers:

- Green (for go) arrows to designate where to start the story (write *start* on the arrows and tell children the arrow means "start")
- Yellow arrows to designate direction or what's next (yellow can mean "proceed with caution")
- Red octagon to designate "stop"—here is where we stop the story

Consistency in colors (matching stoplight signals) helps with remembering. We help children understand and recognize story patterns and structures when we use visual aids and graphic organizers—and we do so playfully.

Found in this section are ideas about how to organize stories for young children so their retelling experiences are supportive and positive. I offer graphic organizer examples and directions for use under specific types of books. Many of the organizational structures may be used across the categories (such as story maps or storyboards). Organizers in the circle book category are pretty limited to circle stories, but otherwise one can use just about any format for any book if needed.

Concept Books

Making story-retelling props for alphabet and counting books may be more trouble than it's worth because one can find alphabet and counting games pre-made and on the Internet. Instead, we find a retelling focus more on concept stories. In table R.1 I list organizers, book examples, and directions.

Table R.1 Two Organizers for Concept Stories

Organizer Book Example	Materials	Directions
Story Key *Brown Bear, Brown Bear* by Bill Martin Jr.	• Colored paper, Unifix cubes • Beads (with safety in mind: large wooden or pony beads) and child-safe cord or string for beads	Colors in the book's endpapers serve as a key. Create a page with color bars or use a stack of Unifix cubes or colored animal icons (or even colored pony beads on a bracelet or necklace) to help the child know what comes next in the sequence. With early retellers, use props and the key. More experienced retellers may retell using only the key.
Story on a Tube (or Tower) *Feelings* by Aliki *The Feelings Book* by Todd Parr	• Long cardboard tube (from wrapping paper) • Velcro • Pictures or icons representing the story sequence and content (you may find Aliki's old books to cut apart for pictures), mounted on card stock and laminated	Cover a long cardboard tube with colored paper and use clear contact paper to protect the paper covering. Add Velcro dots or squares. Place pictures on the dots before the child retells (to serve as prompts in the retelling), or provide the child with pictures so he may reconstruct the plot during story retelling, depending on the experience of the reteller.

Circle Stories

Retell circle stories in a circle format by acquiring or creating a circle and using the perimeter as the graphic organizer—ending up where you began. This is a very physical, concrete way to help children see that stories sometimes come in circles. In table R.2, suggested organizers and stories are provided with brief directions.

Table R.2 Graphic Organizers and Visual Aids for Circle Stories

Organizer Book Example	Materials	Directions
Story Pie *If You Give a Mouse a Cookie* (and other related stories) by Laura Numeroff *Two Mice* by Sergio Ruzzier (as in chapter 7)	• 2 pizza rounds (or cake decorating cardboard rounds), 12, 14, or 16 inches in diameter • Pictures or icons, mounted on card stock and laminated • Clear contact paper • Paper fasteners	Space pictures of key plot events equally around the perimeter of the base circle. Do not use Velcro; instead, make the pictures permanent by either drawing or using glue. If you've glued pictures on the base circle, cover them with contact paper so that when the top circle rotates, the pictures remain. Have you noticed that the topics of four of Numeroff's books are circle shaped? Consider creating the top circle to look like a cookie, donut, pancake, or muffin top—reflecting your book choice. I always write the title of the book on the top circle. Cut a pie shape out of the top circle, sized for revealing only one picture at a time when the circles are stacked. Connect the two circles with a paper fastener. Placing a washer between the circles (all of which are held together by a paper fastener) helps with the rotation.
Story in a Bucket *There's a Hole in the Bucket* (also a song; three versions in print at this writing)	• Bucket or plastic pail with a good circle-shaped rim • Velcro • Pictures or icons, mounted on card stock and laminated	I use black permanent marker to depict a hole in the bucket. Using pictures or a combination of pictures and the real thing (straw, for example), evenly space the Velcro and pictures around the bucket, close to the rim. Use with pictures in place for the child who needs them; remove pictures and have children retell by providing sequence and attaching pictures as appropriate.

(continued on next page)

(continued from previous page)

Organizer Book Example	Materials	Directions
Story Under the Umbrella *Rain* by Manya Stojic	• Child's very safe plastic umbrella • Velcro • Pictures or icons, mounted on card stock and laminated	Decide how you want children to use the umbrella. Do they stand inside of it or outside of it to retell? Using a child's safe umbrella, place Velcro dots or squares on the lower inside of the umbrella so that when the child stands with it open and looks forward and upward, he can retell the story, or on the outside of the umbrella if you want the umbrella stationary (on the floor), so that she stands on the outside of it to retell. Place the reverse Velcro piece on the picture or icon. When retelling is new for children, have all pictures in place before the child begins. By starting with the umbrella open and looking front and center, the child begins retelling. With a little turn and the helpful arrows pointing the way, the next in the sequence is revealed. Let more experienced retellers put the pieces on the umbrella while retelling.
Story in the Round *Bear Has a Story to Tell* by Philip Stead	• Hula hoop or inflatable child's swimming pool • Velcro • Pictures or icons, mounted on card stock and laminated • Finger puppets	Attach Velcro dots and related pictures (or finger puppets) to the hoop to assist children in retelling. In a larger group setting, distribute finger puppets to children and have them come up and place them around the hula hoop when the bear is conversing and helping them.

Cumulative (Add-on) Stories

Cumulative stories are part of our folkloric tradition. Several cumulative story books that represent songs such as *I Know an Old Lady Who Swallowed a Fly* and *The Giant Turnip* have many versions available by authors and illustrators today. We find the cumulative pattern in the more contemporary books *The Napping House* (Wood 1984) and Rohmann's *My Friend Rabbit* (2007). In table R.3, several cumulative tales are used as examples, but many of these organizers can apply to any type of story.

Table R.3 Organizers Applied to Add-on Stories

Organizer / Book Example	Materials	Directions
Story on a Puzzle *The Very Quiet Cricket* by Eric Carle (as in chapter 6)	• Heavy paper (such as poster paper) • Pictures or icons • Lamination	Cut out strips of poster paper. Cut the strips into unique puzzle pieces, making sure each piece connects to only one other puzzle piece (so the puzzle is self-checking). Glue pictures on each piece in story sequence; laminate. When cutting out the lamination, be sure to cut closely to the puzzle so pieces fit together.
Story on a Clothesline *The House That Jack Built* *Feathers for Lunch* by Lois Ehlert (as in chapter 6)	• Clothesline • Clothespins • Pictures or icons, mounted on card stock and laminated	For simplified retelling, lay out the story pictures on the floor or tabletop. Lay string or clothesline above the pictures and clip to the pictures using clothespins. Allow extra string on each end in case you want to tie the string onto two sturdy chairs so it hangs. (Works well on the floor too.) For more complex story retelling, ask children to clip the pictures to the clothesline while retelling.
Stack a Story *My Friend Rabbit* by Eric Rohmann	• Graduated blocks or boxes • Paper to cover the boxes • Pictures or icons • Clear contact paper	Find boxes or blocks that are stackable. I had some old 1–10 graduated counting blocks made of cardboard—they nest when not in use (Melissa and Doug brand make counting blocks; graduated boxes can be found at hobby stores). First cover the boxes with paper. Next add the pictures in sequence with the first item on the largest box or block. (For *My Friend Rabbit*, I just cut animals out of two old paperbacks.) Make sure to focus on the top ten plot events (if using counting blocks) or the number of key plot events to correlate with the number of boxes or blocks you have. Use clear contact paper to cover the pictures and blocks to give them longevity. Children start at the bottom and retell as they add a smaller block. This is self-checking when using graduated boxes.

(continued on next page)

(continued from previous page)

Organizer Book Example	Materials	Directions
Story on a Stick *The Gingerbread Man* *The Little Old Lady Who Was Not Afraid of Anything* by Linda D. Williams (as in chapters 4 and 5)	• Paint stick, plastic ruler, yardstick or comparable item • Velcro • Pictures or icons, mounted on card stock and laminated	Place Velcro dots on the stick, allowing space for each picture, then place the matching Velcro piece on each picture. For novice retellers, keep all pictures in place. Children may either point to the pictures to retell the story or pull out the correct prop and retell by referencing the stick. Allow experienced retellers to retell stories by adding the pictures to the stick in sequence.
Story in a Bag *I Know an Old Lady Who Swallowed a Fly* *Fat Cat* by Margaret Reed MacDonald *The Greedy Python* by Eric Carle (book and CD) *Mr. Grumpy's Outing* by John Burningham *One Dog Canoe* by Mary Casanova	• Bag, plastic container, box, or large envelope • Pictures or icons mounted on card stock and laminated	Create a picture of the "thing" that eats or destroys items in the story, and size or adapt this thing or person to fit the container as its belly. Make the mouth have direct access to the belly, where pictures that are eaten will collect (and can be stored until the next retelling or spit out/ sneezed up by the animal). Children enjoy seeing what accumulates in the belly, so if you can, make a belly window (cut a circle and cover with clear plastic or a page protector so children can watch the items accumulate inside). For canoe or boat cumulative tales: put all characters (toys or finger puppets or pictures) in a toy or handcrafted canoe (or may be created with poster paper and a plastic container). Better yet, get a seaworthy toy canoe and plastic toys for retelling at the water (sensory) table. The canoe is the container for the story.
The Combo *Chicken Little* by Rebecca Emberley and Ed Emberley	Story on a string or stick and story in a bag	Collect props. On the string or stick, add laminated icons of characters to serve as sequence reminders. Create a fox bag (see directions for story in a bag). Once the child has retold the story with all the characters present, the fox "bag" swallows them all up and then sneezes and spits them out again. Works well with tongue depressor puppets that children can make (the Emberleys' art is inspiring), finger or hand puppets, or toys.

Patterned Stories

Stories with patterns are predictable for young children, and most of them have been with us for many years. Our culture embraced them, and we pass them down from one generation to the next. In table R.4, I suggest mixing the visual arts with animal props to support the retelling of *Hattie and the Fox*. Using the visual arts for story retelling requires some planning, but the payoff is huge. Children are enraptured over the emergence of a picture and story right in front of their eyes. In the story path, children may illustrate parts of the story. As long as we all are informed about the pictures and what they represent (labels help keep the pictures true to their intent), anyone can retell a story illustrated by children in the class.

Table R.4 Two Ways to Organize Stories with Patterns

Organizer / Book Example	Materials	Directions
The Visual Arts + Props *Hattie and the Fox* by Mem Fox	• Main animal props or puppets • Large drawing paper • Marker/s	The cumulative tale lends itself to drawing a picture over the course of the retelling. Hattie (hen) warns the other farm animals about the fox, but they don't really pay attention until the end. Use puppets or toys to enact as a group with teacher direction several times before putting children in charge of the retelling. With the picture drawing and the props at hand, the pattern is to tell about new fox characteristics in view, then repeat each animal's "ho hums." Both art and props serve as reminders of the pattern in the book.
Story Path *Three Bears* *Three Billy Goats* *Three Pigs* *Little Red Riding Hood* *Little Red Hen*	• Large butcher paper or roll-out colored paper • Markers • Lamination	Create a path on roll-out paper that meanders from the left and right side of the width of the paper. Draw pictures (or have children illustrate) on one side then the other side of the path—but make sure the pictures are illustrated in clear sequences. Make the pathway as long or as short as you wish, as long as the key ideas are represented. An easy example is the *Three Pigs*: the path could show the pigs first; then the three houses clearly illustrated out of straw, wood, and brick; a wolf and flattened straw house; then flattened wood house; then all three little pigs (depending on your version) huddled in the house of brick; finally, a black pot and a wolf round out the happy (depending on who you are) ending. The child walks down the path, and as she journeys, pictures next to the path prompt the child with sequence and key plot events.

Narrative Stories (Fiction)

In table R.5, I suggest a storyboard (which in Theo's case is really two story strips) and a popular story-on-a-string organizer. In the storyboard structure, the teacher makes a linear strip with windows or frames, and children add characters or key events while retelling.

Table R.5 Two Organizing Structures for Narrative Text

Organizer Book Example	Materials	Directions
Storyboard *Theo's Mood* by Maryann Cocca-Leffler (as in chapter 5)	• Construction or craft paper • Pictures (hand drawn or pulled from online) • Author's color sheet fom her website • Velcro • Lamination	The story has two big plot sequences: one at school (six frames) and one at Theo's home (six frames). Create a story strip for each plot sequence. Put six frames on the first strip and six on the second. Using different colored papers, create the big plot event that led to the mood expressed by each character. Print a copy of the author's "Color Your Mood" page: https://docs.google.com/file/d/0B1X0nD-2djsnhcWVqanE2ejkyRXc/edit?pref=2&pli=1. Use Wite-Out on the mouth for Theo, then make additional copies of Theo with no mouth. Make a copy of each character on colored paper that matches each plot event. Create Theo's mood to fit each plot sequence on the storyboard. Color-code each frame on the storyboard to make it self-checking. Place the picture of the character on the storyboard event causing the mood (in sequence) while retelling.
Story on a Rope *The Saggy Baggy Elephant* by Jackson and Jackson *Do You Want to be My Friend?* by Eric Carle (as in chapter 5)	• Substantial rope (for a group) • Heavy string (for individuals) • Pictures or icons, mounted on card stock and laminated • Velcro (optional)	Make knots on the rope or string that equal the number of picture cards in the plot sequence. Make sure there is ample spacing between pictures. You can add Velcro dots to the knots and the pictures if you wish. Children can lay the picture on or near the knot. To prompt sequence, teachers arrange pictures on the rope prior to child's retelling, and children use the rope with pictures to retell the story. For more challenging retelling, children add pictures to the knots while retelling.

Calendar and Other Timeline Stories

Some stories are told across time. I find that older preschoolers and kindergarteners love playing with the calendar, so retelling with a pretend monthly calendar, clock, or an outdated yearly calendar can motivate a retelling.

Although these stories are delightful for preschoolers and retelling, I would begin with less detail and expect more general retellings and essentially ignore the time in early retellings. Time is an extra detail of the story. Children who understand concepts of time notice the time element in stories. Gauge children's understandings and provide opportunities to play with calendars and clocks in the house or pretend school center. As children draw nearer to kindergarten entry or when they are in the kindergarten, consider small-group work with stories that include more educational focus on the passage of time. In Table R.6, I provide four examples with directions.

Table R.6 Organizing Stories Using Calendars and Clocks

Organizer Book Example	Materials	Directions
Week *Today Is Monday* by Eric Carle	• One-week calendar • Pictures or icons, mounted on card stock and laminated • Velcro	Set up the one-week calendar to make it easy for children to retell. This is a song, so I suggest singing it instead of telling. Once children have the days of the week memorized, the food is the most difficult thing to remember, thus the visual aids should focus on the food. Place a picture or icon of the food listed in each day in story sequence. Sing the story (it repeats) and point to the visual aid. If the child knows the sequence, have him retell by adding the icons to the week's calendar.
Month *Counting Chickens* by Polly Alakija (as in chapter 7)	• One-month calendar • Pictures or icons, mounted on card stock and laminated • Tongue depressors, attached to each picture	This has a lot of props, so the child will need to be able to manage the props and the concept of time. Having a container for each grouping of props makes it possible to move groups around and keep with the story when retelling. I suggest counting and grouping before retelling to check to make sure all props are there (and for the counting experience).
Year *A House for Hermit Crab* by Eric Carle	• Year-at-a-glance calendar, laminated • Pictures or icons, mounted on card stock and laminated	Create icons to represent key events for each month. With Velcro, attach icons to calendar. Children retell the story by pointing, if they're novices, or by adding the icons to the calendar in sequence if experienced.

(continued on next page)

(continued from previous page)

Organizer Book Example	Materials	Directions
Time (kindergarten) *The Grouchy Ladybug* by Eric Carle	• 16" circle • Black construction paper clock hands, laminated • Plastic ladybug • Pictures of animals in the story, mounted on card stock and laminated • Black felt or construction paper • Velcro	Time is simply an organizing structure in the telling of this story, which has many concepts. Make a clock with laminated construction paper hands. Add icons representing plot sequence under each number on the clock to align with plot and timing in the book. The story begins and ends at nighttime, so begin retelling by putting the ladybug on the black paper or felt at the beginning. Fly ladybug over to 5:00, the first icon of the friendly ladybug eating aphids on a leaf, to start the story. Moving through each hour and animal, use clock hands and the ladybug to point to each one to retell, ending back at the nighttime spot. To simplify, don't use clock hands, only the bug.

Props for Story Retelling

In early childhood, story-retelling props serve as magnets as they engage children in "becoming" the story. When I use toys as props, I begin by conducting a search, and if I don't already have the item, I borrow it to gauge how children respond before purchasing it. Children love puppets, and classrooms need depth in puppet choices. Puppets should be rotated in and out, loaned to the class next door, stored in boxes or tubs so they are fresh, and replaced when favorites wear out or go missing. Storing puppets with retelling materials helps keep the materials and puppets fresh—one reason inexpensive finger puppets are helpful for story retelling.

I notice that when children have props, they will both enact and retell, often switching back and forth. They will go into character, drop out into the narrator's voice, then at times, will drop out altogether to have a conversation with the audience.

Table R.7 is a listing of props used in this book along with information about where I sourced them. In table R.8 I share where I found pictures and patterns to adapt for my own finger and hand puppets.

Table R.7 Sources for Props Used in the Book

Item	Description/notes	Company
Plush animal finger and hand puppets	Purchased in bulk only (typically 12 to the package)	Oriental Trading Company
Plastic snake and neon green mice	Sold at Halloween time as seasonal goods	
Wind-up mice	Sold in bulk (12 to a package)	
Plastic troll finger puppets	Used as props for *Little Rabbit Foo Foo*	
Piñata and miscellaneous party items	Used as props for the book *Fiesta*	
3 pigs finger puppets	Also includes house finger puppet and mother pig finger puppet	Amazon.com
Plush animal and people finger puppets	Sold 10–12 per package	
Audubon plush birds	Sounds recorded by Cornell Lab of Ornithology	
Outdated/discontinued Audubon plush birds	I purchased 3 discontinued Audubon plush birds from guatemike and received prompt service (used with *Feathers for Lunch*)	eBay
***Little Red Hen*, whale puppets**	Folkmanis puppets	The Books Vine for Children Barnes & Noble
***Five Little Monkeys* finger puppets**	Merry Makers brand	Barnes & Noble
Hand puppets: 3 pigs, 3 bears, *Three Billy Goats Gruff*	Packaged as sets	Lakeshore Learning
Storytelling lapboard, glove, and Velcro-backed characters and setting pieces	Quick, easy, durable staples for centers	
Flannel board and felt materials	*Very Hungry Caterpillar* and *Brown Bear*	
Hand puppets: 3 bears	Manhattan Toy Company	Toys "R" Us
Hand puppet: fairy	Used in *Little Rabbit Foo Foo*	
String a farm	Alex brand name; used as props for *Old MacDonald Had a Farm*	Walmart Target
Additional props	Such as the balloons, squirrel, and bird in *Bernice Gets Carried Away*; check party supply section	Hobby Lobby (or most craft or party supply stores)

Table R.8 Sources for Patterns and Materials for Hand-Made Props Used in the Book

Item	Description/notes	Company
Craft supplies	Tongue depressors, colored clothespins, soft roping, large buttons, felt, burlap, etc., paper cutters for circles and other shapes, craft paper	Michaels Hobby Lobby Other craft or fabric stores
Finger and hand puppets photographs	A Google search brings many options	Various designs on Etsy and Pinterest
Elephant child-sized hand puppet	Used as a prop for *Little Elliot, Big Family*	Jessica Peck's elephant and directions on her BlogSpot inspired Elliot the Elephant (free instructions online)
Various animal finger puppets	Mostly used as props for *Bernice Gets Carried Away*	Oh Baby (free instructions online)
Fox finger puppet	Inspired the fox I created for *Bernice Gets Carried Away*	Lindy Brown sells these beautiful puppets made out of wool (I made a felt adaptation based on the photograph)

Finding Just the Right Puppet

Following in table R.9 are additional resources for puppets for those who are looking for unique puppets, want to increase their puppetry stock, or just wish to explore.

Table R.9 Sources for Puppets

Item	Description/notes	Company
Puppets	This website offers puppets for sale (see especially their "Little Puppets" for child-sized hands)—the most comprehensive resource on puppetry I've seen in one place.	Folkmanis
Finger puppet sets	Lovely hand-knitted finger puppets from Peru sold in classic story sets	Global Handmade Hope (sells fair trade items)
Knitted finger puppets	Hand-knitted finger puppets from Peru sold in bulk. You don't know what you'll get when you order, but the puppets are delightful.	Sanyork
ECE puppets, stages, and related items	Hand puppets and theaters for ECE	Lakeshore Learning Childcraft/School Specialty
Hand puppets	Hand puppets	Manhattan Toy Company
Puppets and theaters	Hand puppets, sets, and theaters	Melissa and Doug
Large selection of puppets and related items	Hand and finger puppets, marionettes, Folkmanis puppets, accessories, professional puppets	The Puppet Store
Large selection of puppets and related items	This site has *everything* in puppets, but it also has more ready-made puppet sets (in book sets and sometimes with a book). "My First Puppets" are washable.	Puppet U

Glossary

abstraction principle. Anything in a set is counted and is included in the set, whether the set contains the same types of objects or different types of objects.

add-on story. *See* cumulative story.

approximation. The mistakes, miscues, or misconceptions that ensue when learners first encounter new information and try to apply their new knowledge. These approximations help teachers know how to focus teaching.

authentic assessment. Documenting, analyzing, and making decisions based on what children do in their day-to-day work and play; teachers assess while children are engaged in play, interacting, learning, and other typical activities; data include children's drawings and other work samples or teacher checklists, observations, anecdotal notes, and other tools completed in context of children's classroom engagement.

book acting. Another way to conduct story retelling. Children act out the book and in essence retell the story through acting. In preschool, teachers often act as the director of the play and heavily support children in sequencing the play, prompting lines, and encouraging next steps.

cardinality. A construct that identifies the last item counted in a set as the total or number quantity.

circle story. A plot structure used to organize the sequence of events: the story begins and ends in the same place, typically after having a list of adventures or objects or locations.

comprehension. Understanding what is read; making meaning either from reading the text (reading comprehension) or hearing the spoken words (listening comprehension).

conceptual understanding. Deep and elaborative meaning. A behavioral display of depth of knowledge through accurate explanations, telling why, relating cause and effect, and applying knowledge through illustrations, model-making, graphic organizers, stories, and play episodes, for example.

concrete. Used in early childhood education to mean the real thing; a concrete item representing the word *tree* is the actual tree—not a picture or a toy tree—an authentic tree.

content. Knowledge or information associated with a topic, theme, discipline, or project.

context. Environment or setting in which one is situated. When applied to reading, contextual cues are those words surrounding the word or phrase (what) one is reading.

cumulative story. A plot structure used to organize the sequence of events in the story by adding one more character, event, or thing in the sequence. Also known as an add-on book.

developmentally appropriate practice (DAP). A research-based position that advocates for educating young children using approaches that are based on what we know about early childhood education and how children learn and develop. (See position statement at www.naeyc.org.)

dialogic reading. An interactive reading strategy characterized by teachers selecting a book with rich words, introducing the book, asking questions during and after reading that elicit more than yes or no answers, and intentionally responding to children's answers that either validate or elevate their thinking. Dialogic reading has been demonstrated to work especially well with regard to vocabulary development. Parental involvement (through training in dialogic reading strategies) increases impact.

differentiation. Teachers' use of strategies to meet children's individual learning needs and strengths. Teachers design strategies based on their understandings of children's developmental levels, knowledge of how young children learn, and task analysis of content/procedures/concepts.

direct teaching. *See* explicit teaching.

earth and space science. Includes the study of the biosphere, the geosphere, the atmosphere, and the hydrosphere—weather, seasons, rocks, shells, soil, sand, pebbles, shadows, sky, rainbows, sun, moon, stars, water, ice, snow, and clouds.

elements of story or narrative text. The components of fictional stories, typically considered as character, setting, plot, theme, style, tone, and point of view. Symbolization, which more often is found in text for older children, is considered an element of literature. A story's structure, conflict or problem, and the resolution of that problem (and similarly a story's goal to be achieved and the achievement of the goal) are sometimes considered elements of literature but most often are considered the substance of plot.

emotional domain. An area of learning that pertains to feelings: identifying one's and others' feelings, understanding what causes certain feelings to happen, coping strategies, self-regulation of feelings, and managing one's feelings and responding to others' emotions in socially acceptable ways, for example.

enactive. Acting with toys, props, puppets, or with one's own body; becoming the object or experience through acting, sometimes with manipulatives.

engineering. Designing things to meet people's needs or wants; because design is core to engineering, we typically encourage children to create simple designs, then carry out their plans.

explicit teaching. A direct, to-the-point, and precise method of teaching often employed when providing content, teaching a skill, or informing. Teaching and learning is structured and orchestrated by the teacher to provide information. Also known as direct teaching.

exploration. Children tinker, play, interact, observe, test, and/or investigate, and in the process, learn about the item they are exploring.

expository text. Nonfiction writing.

expressive language (*or* vocabulary). The spoken word; putting thoughts together to produce spoken words. Young children typically demonstrate expressive language after they develop receptive language.

factual knowledge. The defining, basic, core information one holds of a concept.

fluency. Reading text accurately, quickly, smoothly, and expressively; supports reading for comprehension.

formative assessment. Assessing while children are engaged in an authentic project or learning objective to inform teachers of children's learning and thus inform them of next steps in teaching.

frequently read words. Words that most often appear in text, such as *the*, *a*, *and*, and *of*. These words are early sight words for emergent readers: the frequently read words are recognized as whole words rather than by stopping to sound out each letter in the word, which increases fluency and likewise comprehension.

gist. The essence, main point, substance, or core meaning of a story or idea.

guided play. Conceptualized by Weisberg, Hirsh-Pasek, and Golinkoff (2013) to describe a teaching strategy for young children that capitalizes on children's penchant for learning through play experiences. Teachers plan for and intentionally create small-group learning scenarios that first engage children in a play experience before teachers guide the play toward learning objectives by posing questions, for example.

iconic representation. Using a symbol or small picture that embodies the meaning or essence of the object.

implicit teaching. An indirect method of teaching: teachers set the stage for learning by posing problems, asking questions, and creating environments that will facilitate inquiry, application of concepts, practice, or guided play or discovery.

inquiry. In simple terms, asking a question and finding out the answer through a person or source such as a dictionary; in more complex terms, investigating a phenomena or problem by conducting an investigation or project to discover answers and communicate results to others.

intentional teaching *or* intentionality in teaching. Implementing or carrying out interactions and responses to children with purpose and reason.

interactive reading. A strategy used in read-alouds where teachers plan before-, during-, and after-reading interactions with children that promote understanding of story and vocabulary development. Several specific methods, such as shared reading and dialogic reading, are considered to fall under the interactive reading umbrella.

life sciences. A focus on all living things. Life sciences involve a study of the patterns in living things, how they relate to each other, and how they grow and behave.

map *or* mapping. Using graphic representation of the story either to help children understand the structure of story or to serve as a prop for supporting story retelling; refers to how the parts of story relate to one another as revealed in the plot. Examples include but are not limited to the following organizational formats: rhyming patterns, repetitive text, beginning-middle-end, circle, and add-on or cumulative.

mathematize. A way of looking at the world from a mathematics perspective; turning a story or situation in the classroom into a math problem or scenario by noticing the math and posing a problem.

modeling. Teachers play on the power of imitation by demonstrating. Modeling story retelling with props and other teacher-made story structures assists children in understanding the expectations of how to retell a story.

narrative text. Fiction writing.

nominal. Describes or represents something such as an address, a phone number, or a numeral printed on a T-shirt.

numeral. The symbol that denotes number.

one-to-one correspondence. Matching one object to another object; this skill is at the core of associating one number word with one object.

oral language complexity. How one organizes and communicates the structure of and elaboration on a topic, a story, or an idea. Language that includes description, explanation (*because, so*), and organization (*first, and then*) demonstrates more complexity than language that simply states events without description, explanation, or organization.

order-irrelevance principle. The sequence of counting objects in a set does not matter as long as each object in the set is counted just one time; objects can be counted in any order.

ordinals. The vocabulary that designates order, such as *first*, *second*, *third*, and so on. They are useful for young children to learn once they secure the sense of number.

pair-share. A cooperative learning strategy where children pair up with each other and take turns sharing. In story retelling, pair-share can take on the form of taking turns to share (or retell) parts of the story in sequence.

participative stories. Stories in which teachers create interactive components for children to enact, imitate, and/or tell with expression during reading. Children are taught sound effects and repeating lines, for example, to supply on cue during the read-aloud, which serve to engage children and build story-retelling skills in group formats.

part-whole relationship. Refers to being able to take numbers apart into smaller sets and have the awareness that the smaller sets (the parts) together equal the whole. This concept also teaches children that there are lots of different ways to represent one number.

pedagogy. The art, knowledge, skill, and practice of teaching.

peritextual features. In books this refers to all the words and pictures that surround the story or expository text: examples are the book cover, end papers, title page, and dedication.

physical science. The study of physics and chemistry. In the physical sciences, we learn overarching concepts of cause and effect. Selected examples of physical science in ECE are studies of forces, ramps, pathways, inclines, cooking, bubbles, light, color, pulleys, ropes, and magnets.

plot. The main events in a story specifically arranged in a sequence by the author.

pretend reading. Children pick up a book and pretend to read. They may or may not have previously heard the story, but one can tell if the child is developing early literacy skills by watching how she holds the book, turns a page, uses the pictures as visual aids in retelling the story, and understands if she should go to the end of the book before finishing.

props. In story retelling or enacting, those items that help us retell or enact, such as dolls representative of book characters, toy farm animals or puppets that serve as animals in *Old MacDonald Had a Farm*, or toy cars or dishes, for example.

psychosocial development theory. Based on Erickson's work (1993), the theory has implications on early childhood teachers: to provide safe and predictable environments so children will grow trustful in infancy; to offer opportunities for choices and independence so children will grow autonomous in toddlerhood; to provide environments that spark inquiry and investigation so children can take initiative in preschool and kindergarten; and to offer opportunities to carry out plans so children may grow industrious while in the early childhood years.

real graphs. A graph made of real things: people, shoes, stuffed bears brought from home, favorite apples. These graphs are the embodiment of the concrete phase of teaching and learning. Young children are interested in real things, so they attend to them. They are engaged with real objects, so they learn about graphing concepts through engagement.

receptive language (or vocabulary). Understanding what is said; processing the spoken language, interpreting and/or comprehending it, then integrating it into one's language and meaning repertoire. Young children typically develop receptive language (measured by asking children to point or select a picture or prop) before they demonstrate expressive language.

responsive teaching. Capitalizing on teacher-child interactions, one listens and learns from the child, and thoughtfully responds by providing that which the child needs to nurture or advance learning.

scaffold(ing). A supportive process teachers provide to children while learning. When a task or learning endeavor is not attainable to the child, teachers provide assistance so the child can complete it successfully. As the child becomes more independent in her efforts, the teacher eases back and slowly withdraws support so the child can move toward independent performance.

self-awareness. An awareness of one's own personality, likes, dislikes, strengths, and weaknesses. Young children are developing self-awareness in preschool and kindergarten.

semantic cueing. While reading (or listening), one makes meaning of text (comprehends) by attending to what is read (or said) in the entire passage, using context to support meaning making.

shared reading. An interactive reading strategy characterized by using large print (such as Big Books or large-printed charts) visible to everyone in the group and focusing on text as well as content through interactive strategies.

social domain. An area of learning that pertains to developing skills, concepts, and responsibilities that facilitate children in successful perceptions, interpretations, and responses in social situations. Developing an understanding of cultural and conventional norms and expectations and interacting with others in accordance with these beliefs and values.

social-emotional domains. A combination of the social domain with the emotional domain. Because both domains are interdependent and related, educators typically put them together for the sake of convenience, whereas psychologists and others might separate the domains to clarify terminology and offer more specific and direct intervention strategies.

stable order rule. The order of the number words in counting always remains the same or stable (one, two, three, four).

story map. *See* map.

story retelling. The act of conveying or sharing any story to others after either hearing, reading, or experiencing it. In early childhood educational settings, the concept and process of story retelling is twofold: what teachers do to facilitate and support children's story retelling and what children do when they retell a story.

structure of story. Organization of the story; how the author reveals the story's characters, setting, plot, theme, and so on. Beginning, middle, end (as found in fiction or biography); circle, cumulative, calendar, and other as best describes the story (related: map or mapping).

subitize. Recognizing how many are in a group without counting. Subitizing is helpful for counting on and is something of a shortcut that allows children to have flow in mathematical thinking and computing.

summative assessments. A final or ending assessment at the culmination of a project or learning experience. Summative assessments may "sum up" learning in one assessment.

symbolic representation. Using symbols such as colored beads, blocks, letters, numerals, words, and sentences to stand for an object, a place, an experience, a person, or an event in a story.

syntactic cueing. Using knowledge of the structure of written language to make meaning out of text. Frequent exposure to literature assists children in internalizing how language is structured in stories and subsequently helps them with gathering meaning while listening and later while reading.

text-to-self connections. Making connections between the text and one's own life experiences through teacher modeling and also teacher facilitation. It is believed to be the most effective of the connections young children make with texts that result in gaining meaning and making associations.

think-out-loud strategy. A teaching strategy that involves thinking out loud while doing a task or procedure or problem solving—the teacher is modeling how she thinks. This is often used in reading instruction, especially with sounding out words or discerning words in context.

Tier One words. Words that are basic and frequently spoken, typically words we use while talking and especially when working with young children (such as *cat*).

Tier Two words. More sophisticated words often found in literature, including children's literature—for example, the word *sow* instead of *pig* (or more specifically, a mother pig).

transactional theory of reading. A theory developed by Louise Rosenblatt (1994) that draws from the sociocultural theorists. Rosenblatt believed that higher levels of textual understanding are acquired when a group can interact and exchange perspectives with one another. Doing so provides opportunities for group members to transcend their own individual understanding.

verbatim memory. Remembering a passage word for word. Typically not considered as "lasting" as gist.

visual aid. A picture, an icon, or a drawing that helps us remember key elements of a story while retelling it.

wordless picture books. Books with only pictures or mostly pictures that include few, if any, words. When teachers use these books for read-alouds and story retelling, they plan ahead how it will be read by choosing their own focus vocabulary words and interpretations of the pictures.

zone of proximal development. By starting with what is known to the child and helping the child move toward understanding or a skill unknown to him, we are most effective when teaching within the range between what children can do alone and what they can do with assistance in the move toward independence. This range is known as the zone of proximal development (developed by Vygotsky).

Story-Retelling Forms

Form 8.1 Observation of Story Retelling in Free Play

Child's Name:	Book:
Props:	Context:

Indicators	Observations
Observe and document one or more of the following: • Uses story-related vocabulary • Retells or enacts story-related plot events • Adds creative innovations to the story, such as changing or adding new story plot events, new characters, or changes in characters' behavior, props, or setting • Creates new stories with story props representing characters • Includes characters or events in his own play scenarios • Other:	(Document indicators with observational details, children's quotes, play summaries, and/or original innovations on the story through creative play.)

Notes:

Analysis: What do these data tell you about the child's use of story? Vocabulary usage? Integration of the child's life into the story (or vice versa)? Creative storytelling? Other?

Form 8.2 Documenting Story Retelling through Acting: Group Enactment Form

Instructions: Enter the actors' names in the form below. Document time and interactions as they happen on the form in a linear way, using additional forms as needed. This form gives the user a visual example of interaction as it happens by noting times in which new interaction streams (adapted with permission from Pamela Oken-Wright, personal communication, February 26, 1999).

Book:				Date & Time:
Context:				
Child's Name Role Played	**Child's Name Role Played**	**Child's Name Role Played**	**Child's Name Role Played**	**Teacher Reflections**

Notes about taking direction, participation, expression, social awareness, enjoyment, playfulness/creativity, accuracy in meaning of lines, and use of props (if applicable):

Form 8.3 Class Checklist: Fingerplays, Rhymes, Songs, and Participative Story Retelling

Instructions: List the title/date of the fingerplay, rhyme, song, or interactive story. List also children's names and check (✔) if children demonstrate the indicator. Write notes and observations as needed.

Book:					Date:
Children's Names	**Learning Process:** *Participates; Shows Enjoyment and Interest*	**Knows Words and Tunes**	**Includes Actions or Uses Props or Visual Aids**	**Teacher Prompt Needed**	**Observations** What stands out in child's learning process? Knowledge of words and tunes? Actions or props?

Comprehension & Vocabulary Questions:

Form 8.4 Checklist for Retelling a Concept Book

Instructions: List the title of the concept book and the concept it addresses. List children's names and check (✔) if children demonstrate the indicator. Record observations. If desired, either add the indicator "Sequence" to the checklist or note it in the observations when children are ready for this indicator to identify if sequence is applied in retelling.

Book:

Concept Addressed:

List Children's Names	Enjoys / Holds Interest in Retelling	Accurate Use of Concept	Accurate Use of Props or Visual Aids	Teacher Prompt Needed	Observations & Notes

Comprehension & Vocabulary Questions:

Notes on How the Child Sequences the Retelling:

Form 8.5 Story Retelling: Levels and Observations (adapted from children's development in creative story dictation (Chen and McNamee 2007, with permission from Corwin)

Directions: Circle the indicator that best describes the overall retelling. Check if prompts are provided. Include observations or teacher notes as relevant to the retelling.

Name:		Date:	
Book:			

Select One	Indicators	Check (✔) If Prompted	Child Observations or Teacher Notes
Refusal	Refuses to retell story or speak (no word utterances).		
1–3 words	Speaks one to three words that are not connected to each other but may be relevant to the story.		
Sentence or list	Retells the story in either a sentence or list with little to no plot or action or characterization.		
Undeveloped ideas	Retells a number of undeveloped events, thoughts, concepts, or characters related to the story but lacks the essence, key ideas, central idea, or characters behind a story.		
String of ideas	Retells by stringing together ideas as if telling a story without a central theme or idea; lacks plot, continuity, central characters, and focus.		
Central idea but not fully developed	Retells with a central theme or character or concept but lacks continuity and is not fully developed.		
Main idea prevails	The story includes elements and characters central to the plot where the main idea of the story prevails. The central plot is revealed as a problem or goal.		
Generally accurate	Story retelling is overall accurate. It includes many of the essentials: beginning, middle, and end; problem and solution (or goal and how goal was met); characters; setting (time and place); plot sequence and overall theme; and details.		

Form 8.6 Literature-Based Story-Retelling Checklist and Observations

Instructions:

Context

Provide a brief summary of the child's exposure to the story prior to assessment, such as summarizing the number of times the child has formally practiced retelling the story in a small group and/or informally in play, if observed.

Notes

Add retelling notes as needed.

Indicators of Narrative Story:

Characters

- In the Story Descriptors column, list characters you believe are most important in the retelling.

Setting

- In the Story Descriptors column, list key settings important to the story.

Repeated Lines or Vocabulary

- Are vocabulary or lines repeated in the story—lines that practically identify the story-retelling experience? If so, they should be listed in the Story Descriptors column.

Plot/Sequence of Events/Organization

- Write an outline of key events in the story in the Story Descriptors column. Include vocabulary that demonstrates organizing structures (*because, so, first, next . . .*)

Problem (or goal)

- What is the problem or the goal in the story? List in the Story Descriptors column.

Resolution (or steps taken to meet the goal)

- How is the problem resolved, or how is the goal met? List in the Story Descriptors column.

Teacher Prompts (✔)

Check if prompting is needed. Teachers prompt young children when they request it or when the teacher believes it is needed to support the child. The key is to create positive story-retelling experiences with children so they will continue developing and enjoying retelling experiences.

This Story's Descriptors

Enter information about the story relevant to children's classroom learning experiences.

Child's Story Descriptors

Document children's words or summarize their stories for analysis.

Comprehension Questions

Questions that gather information about whether children understood the story (meanings, themes, big ideas, and/or events).

Inference Questions

Questions that ask the child to draw conclusions based on facts or events in the story. Inference questions go beyond the text and into inferring, a needed skill for reading comprehension strategies later.

Analysis

After documenting the story retelling by collecting data and taking notes, teachers analyze data to understand what story vocabulary is being used, how the child internalizes story structure, meaning, and other indicators of retelling. Overall, recognition of the following can assist in teaching to strengths and nurturing next steps in development:

- What is the child doing well?
- What are next steps in development?
- How might I focus my teaching to play upon the child's strengths and facilitate next steps in children's development as story retellers?
- What themes and patterns are noted as strengths across groups of students or the whole class? How might this inform my next steps in teaching?

(continued from previous page.)

Name: **Date:**

Book:

Context:

Indicators	Check (✔) If Prompted	Story's Descriptors	Child's Descriptors Used While Retelling the Story	Check (✔) If Prompted
Characters				
Setting				
Repeated Lines/Key Vocabulary				
Plot Sequence/ Events/Organization				
Problem or Goal				
Resolution or How Goal Was Met				

Comprehension Questions:

Inference Questions:

Notes:

Form 8.7 Observations of Communication and Oral Language Displayed in Story Retelling (adapted from the terminology used in the New Zealand School Entry Assessment Story Retelling Task, as reported by Riley and Burrell 2007 with permission from the New Zealand Ministry of Education)

Name: **Date:**

Book:

Indicator	Observations
Word choices, vocabulary, and sentence structure	
Expression	
Organization	
Content	
Descriptions	
Other	

Comprehension Check:

Notes:

References

Anderson, Jim, Lyndsay Moffatt, Marianne McTavish, and Jon Shapiro. 2013. "Rethinking Language Education in Early Childhood: Socio-Cultural Perspectives." In *Handbook of Research on the Education of Young Children*, 3rd edition, edited by Olivia N. Saracho with Bernard Spodek, 117–34. New York: Routledge.

Applebee, Arthur N. 1978. *The Child's Concept of Story: Ages Two to Seventeen*. Chicago: University of Chicago Press.

Beauchat, Katherine A., Katrin L. Blamey, and Zoi A. Philippakos. 2012. *Effective Read-Alouds for Early Literacy: A Teacher's Guide for PreK-1*. New York: Guilford.

Beck, Isabel L., Margaret G. McKeown, and Linda Kucan. 2013. *Bringing Words to Life: Robust Vocabulary Instruction*. 2nd ed. New York: Guilford.

Bodrova, Elena, and Deborah J. Leong. 2006. *Tools of the Mind: The Vygotskian Approach to Early Childhood Education*. 2nd ed. Upper Saddle River, NJ: Pearson Merrill Prentice Hall.

Brainerd, C. J., and V. F. Renya. 1993. "Domains of Fuzzy-Trace Theory." In *Emerging Themes in Cognitive Development: Volume 1: Foundations*, edited by Robert Pasnak and Mark L. Howe. New York: Springer.

Bridges, Mindy Sittner, Laura M. Justice, Tiffany P. Hogan, and Shelley Gray. 2012. "Promoting Lower- and Higher-Level Language Skills in Early Education Classrooms." In *Handbook of Early Childhood Education*, edited by Robert C. Pianta, W. Steven Barnett, Laura M. Justice, and Susan M. Sheridan, 177–93. New York: Guilford.

Bruner, Jerome S. 1966. *Toward a Theory of Instruction*. Cambridge, MA: Harvard University Press.

The Center on the Social and Emotional Foundations for Early Learning (CSEFEL). 2006. *Promoting the Social Emotional Competence of Young Children: Facilitator's Guide*. The University of Illinois, Urbana-Champaign. http://csefel.vanderbilt.edu/modules/facilitators-guide.pdf.

Chalufour, Ingrid, and Karen Worth. 2004. *Building Structures with Young Children: Young Scientists Series*. St. Paul, MN: Redleaf.

Chen, Jie-Qi, and Gillian Dowley McNamee. 2007. *Bridging: Assessment for Teaching and Learning in Early Childhood Classrooms, Pre-K–3*. Thousand Oaks, CA: Corwin.

Cole, Luella. 1950/2007. *A History of Education: Socrates to Montessori*. New York: Holt, Rinehart & Winston.

Collaborative for Academic, Social, and Emotional Learning (CASEL). 2013. *The 2013 CASEL Guide: Effective Social and Emotional Learning Programs, Preschool and Elementary School Edition*. Chicago: CASEL.

Copple, Carol, and Sue Bredekamp. 2009. *Developmentally Appropriate Practice in Early Childhood Programs Serving Children from Birth through Age 8*. 3rd ed. Washington, DC: National Association for the Education of Young Children.

Curtis, Deb, and Margie Carter. 2003. *Designs for Living and Learning: Transforming Early Childhood*. St. Paul, MN: Redleaf.

DeVries, Rheta, and Christina Sales. 2011. *Ramps and Pathways: A Constructivist Approach to Physics with Young Children*. Washington, DC: National Association for the Education of Young Children.

Dunn, L. M., and D. M. Dunn. 2007. *Peabody Picture Vocabulary Test*. 4th ed. Minneapolis: Pearson Assessments.

Dunst, Carl J., Andrew Simkus, and Deborah W. Hamby. 2012. "Children's Story Retelling as a Literacy and Language Enhancement Strategy." *CELL Reviews* 5 (2): 1–14. http://www.earlyliteracylearning.org/cellreviews/cell reviews_v5_n2.pdf.

Epstein, Ann S. 2009. *Me, You, Us: Social-Emotional Learning in Preschool*. Ypsilanti, MI: HighScope Press & National Association for the Education of Young Children.

———. 2014. *The Intentional Teacher: Choosing the Best Strategies for Young Children's Learning*. Rev. ed. Washington, DC: National Association for the Education of Young Children & HighScope Press.

Erikson, Erik H. 1993. *Childhood and Society*. New York: W. W. Norton.

Filippinni, Tiziana, and Vea Vecchi, eds. 1996. *I cento linguaggi dei bambini/ The Hundred Languages of Children*. Reggio Emilia, Italy: Reggio Children.

Fleming, Denise. n.d. "Transcript from an interview with Denise Fleming." Reading Rockets. Accessed November 10, 2016, www.readingrockets.org /books/interviews/fleming/transcript.

Fry, Edward. 2011. *1,000 Instant Words: The Most Common Words for Teaching Reading, Writing and Spelling*. Westminster, CA: Teacher Created Resources.

Gartrell, Dan. 2012. *Education for a Civil Society: How Guidance Teaches Young Children Democratic Life Skills.* Washington, DC: National Association for the Education of Young Children.

Gibson, Akimi, Judith Gold, and Charissa Sgouros. 2003. "The Power of Story Retelling." *The Tutor*: Spring 2003. www.nationalserviceresources.gov/file manager/download/learns/spr2003.pdf.

Gonzalez, Jorge E., Sharolyn D. Pollard-Durodola, Deborah C. Simmons, Aaron B. Taylor, Matthew J. Davis, Melissa Fogarty, and Leslie Simmons. 2014. "Enhancing Preschool Children's Vocabulary: Effects of Teacher Talk Before, After, and During Shared Reading." *Early Childhood Research Quarterly* 29 (2): 214–26.

Gonzalez, Norma, Luis C. Moll, and Cathy Amanti, eds. 2005. *Funds of Knowledge: Theorizing Practice in Households, Communities, and Classrooms.* New York: Routledge.

Harris, Justin, Roberta Michnick Golinkoff, and Kathy Hirsh-Pasek. 2011. "Lessons from the Crib for the Classroom: How Children Really Learn Vocabulary." In *Handbook of Early Literacy Research, Vol. 3,* edited by Susan B. Neuman and David K. Dickinson, 49–65. New York: Guilford.

Hart, Betty, and Todd R. Risley. 2003. "The Early Catastrophe: The 30 Million Word Gap by Age 3." *American Educator.* Spring: 4–9. www.aft.org//sites/default/files/periodicals/TheEarlyCatastrophe.pdf.

Hawkins, David. 2002. *The Informed Vision: Essays on Learning and Human Nature.* New York: Algora.

Head Start. 2015. *Head Start Early Learning Outcomes Framework: Ages Birth to Five.* Washington, DC: US Department of Health and Human Services Administration for Children and Families: Office of Head Start. https://eclkc.ohs.acf.hhs.gov/hslc/hs/sr/approach/pdf/ohs-framework.pdf.

Kneidel, Sally. 2015. *Creepy Crawlies and the Scientific Method: More Than 100 Hands-On Science Experiments for Children.* 2nd ed. Golden, CO: Fulcrum.

Kostelnik, Marjorie J., Anne K. Soderman, Alice Phipps Whiren, and Michelle L. Rupiper. 2015. *Developmentally Appropriate Curriculum: Best Practices in Early Childhood Education.* Boston: Pearson.

Krinitz, Esther Nisenthal, and Bernice Steinhardt. 2010. *Memories of Survival.* Washington, DC: Art and Remembrance.

Lionni, Annie. 2007. "Leo Lionni." In *Artist to Artist: 23 Major Illustrators Talk to Children about Their Art*, 50. New York: Philomel.

Malaguzzi, Loris, and Guido Petter. 1996. "Ombralità/Shadowiness." In *I cento linguaggi dei bambini/The hundred languages of children*, edited by Tiziana Filippini and Vea Vecchi, 118–24. Reggio Emilia, Italy: Reggio Children.

Martin, Bill Jr. 1996. "Transcript from an interview with Bill Martin Jr." Reading Rockets. Accessed November 10, 2016, http://www.readingrockets.org/books/interviews/martin/transcript.

McGee, Lea M. 2008. "Book Acting: Storytelling and Drama in the Early Childhood Classroom." In *Literacy and Young Children: Research-Based Practices*, edited by Diane M. Barone and Lesley Mandel Morrow, 157–72. New York: Guilford.

McGee, Lea M., and Judith A. Schickedanz, J. 2007. "Repeated Interactive Read-Alouds in Preschool and Kindergarten." *The Reading Teacher* 60 (8): 742–51.

Moll, Luis C., Cathy Amanti, Deborah Neff, and Norma Gonzalez. 1992/2001. "Funds of Knowledge for Teaching: Using a Qualitative Approach to Connect Homes and Classrooms." *Theory into Practice* 31 (2): 132–41.

Moomaw, Sally. 2013. *Teaching STEM in the Early Years: Activities for Integrating Science, Technology, Engineering, and Mathematics*. St. Paul, MN: Redleaf.

Morrow, Lesley Mandel. 1985. "Retelling Stories: A Strategy for Improving Young Children's Comprehension, Concept of Story Structure, and Oral Language Complexity." *The Elementary School Journal* 85 (5): 646–61.

———. 1986. "Effects of Structural Guidance in Story Retelling on Children's Dictation of Original Stories." *Journal of Reading Behavior* 18 (2): 135–52.

———. 1996. "Story Retelling: A Discussion Strategy to Develop and Assess Comprehension." In *Lively Discussions! Fostering Engaged Reading*, edited by Linda B. Gambrell and Janice F. Almasi, 265–85. Newark, DE: International Reading Association.

———. 2015. *Literacy Development in the Early Years: Helping Children Read and Write*. 8th ed. Boston: Pearson.

Morrow, Lesley Mandel, Kathleen A. Roskos, and Linda B. Gambrell. 2015. *Oral Language and Comprehension in Preschools: Teaching the Essentials*. New York: Guilford.

Munsch, Robert. 1994. "Beginning with Peekaboo: Storytelling as Interaction." *Child Care Information Exchange* 98: 32–34. https://ccie-catalog.s3.amazonaws.com/library/5009832.pdf.

National Council for Teachers of Mathematics (NCTM). 2009. *Focus in Grades PreK-2: Teaching with Curriculum Focal Points*. Reston, VA: NCTM.

———. 2010. *Focus in Kindergarten: Teaching with Curriculum Focal Points*. Reston, VA: NCTM.

NCTM and National Association for the Education of Young Children (NAEYC). 2010. *Early Childhood Mathematics: Promoting Good Beginnings*.

Washington, DC: NAEYC. www.naeyc.org/files/naeyc/file/positions/psmath .pdf.

National Research Council (NRC). 2012. *A Framework for K-12 Science Education: Practices, Crosscutting Concepts, and Core Ideas.* Washington, DC: National Academies Press.

National Science Teachers Association (NSTA). 2014. "NSTA Position Statement: Early Childhood Science Education." *Science and Children* 51 (7): 10–12.

Nelson, Greg. 2007. *Math at Their Own Pace: Child-Directed Activities for Developing Early Number Sense.* St. Paul, MN: Redleaf.

Neuman, Susan B. 2011. "The Challenge of Teaching Vocabulary in Early Education." In *Handbook of Early Literacy Research, Vol. 3*, edited by Susan B. Neuman and David K. Dickinson, 358–72. New York: Guilford.

Neumann-Hinds, Carla. 2007. *Picture Science: Using Digital Photography to Teach Young Children.* St. Paul, MN: Redleaf.

Owocki, Gretchen. 1999. *Literacy through Play.* Portsmouth, NH: Heinemann.

———. 2005. *Time for Literacy Centers: How to Organize and Differentiate Instruction.* Portsmouth, NH: Heinemann.

Paris, Alison H., and Scott G. Paris. 2007. "Teaching Narrative Comprehension Strategies to First Graders." *Cognition and Instruction* 25 (1): 1–44.

Pinnell, Gay Su, and Irene C. Fountas. 2011. *Literacy Beginnings: A Prekindergarten Handbook.* Portsmouth, NH: Heinemann.

Resnick, Lauren B., and Catherine E. Snow. 2009. *Speaking and Listening for Preschool through Third Grade.* Rev. ed. Pittsburgh: The National Center on Education and the Economy and International Reading Association.

Riley, Jeni, and Andrew Burrell. 2007. "Assessing Children's Oral Story Retelling in Their First Year of School." *International Journal of Early Years Education* 15 (2): 181–96.

Rosenblatt, Louise M. 1994. *The Reader, the Text, the Poem: The Transactional Theory of the Literary Work.* Carbondale, IL: Southern Illinois University Press.

Santrock, John W. 2012. *Children.* 12th ed. Boston: McGraw-Hill.

Sipe, Lawrence R. 2008. *Storytime: Young Children's Literary Understanding in the Classroom.* New York: Teachers College Press.

Smith, Susan Sperry. 2013. *Early Childhood Mathematics.* 5th ed. Boston: Pearson.

Spencer, Trina D., Mandana Kajian, Douglas B. Petersen, and Nicholas Bilyk. 2014. "Effects of an Individualized Narrative Intervention on Children's Storytelling and Comprehension Skills." *Journal of Early Intervention* 35 (September 2013): 243–67.

Vygotsky, Lev. 1978. *Mind in Society: The Development of Higher Psychological Processes*. Rev. ed. Boston: Harvard University Press.

———. 1986. *Thought and Language*. Edited by Alex Kozulin. Rev. ed. Cambridge, MA: MIT Press.

Weisberg, Deena Skolnick, Kathy Hirsh-Pasek, and Roberta Michnick Golinkoff. 2013. "Guided Play: Where Curricular Goals Meet Playful Pedagogy." *Mind, Brain, and Education* 7 (2): 104–12.

Welsch, Jodi G. 2008. "Playing within and beyond the Story: Encouraging Book-Related Pretend Play." *The Reading Teacher* 62 (2): 138–48.

Whitehurst, Grover J., David S. Arnold, Jeffery N. Epstein, Andrea L. Angell, Meagan Smith, and Janet E. Fischel. 1994. "A Picture Book Reading Intervention in Day Care and Home for Children from Low-Income Families." *Developmental Psychology* 30 (5): 679–789.

Whitin, David, and Phyllis Whitin. 2004. *New Visions for Linking Literature and Mathematics*. Reston, VA: National Council of Teachers of Mathematics.

Wilburne, Jane M., Jane B. Keat, and Mary Napoli. 2011. *Cowboys Count, Monkeys Measure, and Princesses Problem Solve: Building Early Math Skills through Storybooks*. Baltimore: Paul H. Brookes.

Wood, David, Jerome S. Bruner, and Gail Ross. 1976. "The Role of Tutoring in Problem Solving." *Journal of Child Psychiatry and Psychology* 17 (2): 89–100.

Zevenbergen, Andrea A., and Grover J. Whitehurst. 2003. "Dialogic Reading: A Shared Picture Book Reading Intervention for Preschoolers." In *On Reading Books to Children: Parents and Teachers*, edited by Anne Van Kleeck, Steven A. Stahl, and Eurydice B. Bauer, 177–200. Mahwah, NJ: Lawrence Erlbaum Associates.

Children's Books Referenced in the Text

Aker, Suzanne. 1990. *What Comes in 2's, 3's, and 4's?* Illustrated by Bernie Karlin. New York: Aladdin.

Alakija, Polly. 2014. *Counting Chickens.* London: Frances Lincoln Children's Books.

Aliki. 1986. *Feelings.* New York: Greenwillow Books.

Allen, Kathryn Madeline. 2015. *Show Me Happy.* Park Ridge, IL: Albert Whitman.

Aloian, Molly. 2012. *What Are Bulbs and Roots? (Plants Up Close).* St. Catharines, ON: Crabtree.

Anderson, Sara. 2009. *Numbers.* Seattle: Sara Anderson Children's Books.

Asch, Frank. (1985) 2014. *Moonbear's Shadow.* New York: Aladdin.

Aston, Dianna Hutts. 2012. *A Rock Is Lively.* Illustrated by Sylvia Long. San Francisco: Chronicle.

Baker, Keith. 1999. *Quack and Count.* San Diego: Harcourt Children's Books.

Beaumont, Karen. 2015. *Wild About Us!* Illustrated by Janet Stevens. New York: Houghton Mifflin Harcourt.

Brown, Marc. 2013. *Marc Brown's Playtime Rhymes: A Treasury for Families to Learn and Play Together.* New York: Little, Brown.

Brown, Marcia. 1997. *Stone Soup.* New York: Aladdin.

Bryan, Ashley. 2009. *Ashley Bryan: Words to My Life's Song.* New York: Atheneum Books for Young Readers.

Buckley, Richard. 2015. *The Greedy Python.* Illustrated by Eric Carle. Read by Stanley Tucci. New York: Little Simon.

Bulla, Clyde Robert. 1994. *What Makes a Shadow?* Illustrated by June Otani. New York: HarperCollins.

Bunting, Eve. 2000. *Flower Garden.* Illustrated by Kathryn Hewitt. San Diego: Voyager Books.

Burnie, David. 2008. *Eyewitness: Bird.* New York: DK Publishing.

Burningham, John. 1970. *Mr. Grumpy's Outing.* New York: Henry Holt.

Burris, Priscilla. 2016. *Five Green and Speckled Frogs.* New York: Cartwheel.

Carle, Eric. (1974) 2006. *My Very First Book of Numbers.* New York: Philomel.

———. 1976. *Do You Want to Be My Friend?* New York: HarperCollins.

———. 1984. *The Mixed-Up Chameleon.* New York: HarperCollins.

————. 1990. *The Very Quiet Cricket*. New York: Philomel.

————. 1997. *Today Is Monday*. New York: PaperStar.

————. 1997. *The Very Hungry Caterpillar*. New York: Philomel.

————. 1999. *Grouchy Ladybug*. New York: HarperCollins.

————. 2001. *The Honeybee and the Robber*. New York: Philomel.

————. 2014. *A House for Hermit Crab*. New York: Simon Spotlight.

Casanova, Mary. 2003. *One Dog Canoe*. Illustrated by Ard Hoyt. New York: Square Fish.

Christelow, Eileen. 2010. *Five Little Monkeys Jumping on the Bed*. New York: Clarion Books.

Christian, Peggy. 2008. *If You Find a Rock*. Photographs by Barbara Hirsch Lember. New York: HMH Books for Young Readers.

Cocca-Leffler, Maryann. 2013. *Theo's Mood*. New York: Albert Whitman.

Cronin, Doreen. 2003. *Diary of a Worm*. Illustrated by Harry Bliss. New York: HarperCollins.

Curato, Mike. 2015. *Little Elliot, Big Family*. New York: Henry Holt.

Davick, Linda. 2015. *Say Hello!* New York: Beach Lane Books.

Dean, James. 2015. *Pete the Cat: Five Little Pumpkins*. Illustrated by James Dean. New York: HarperCollins.

Dicmas, Courtney. 2013. *Harold Finds a Voice*. Swindon, UK: Child's Play International.

Douglas, Lloyd G. 2002. *What Is a Wheel and Axle?* New York: Rosen Book Works.

Ehlert, Lois. 1990. *Feathers for Lunch*. San Diego: Harcourt, Brace.

Emberley, Ed, and Anne Miranda. 1997. *Glad Monster, Sad Monster: A Book about Feelings*. New York: LB Kids.

Emberley, Rebecca. 2009. *Chicken Little*. Illustrated by Ed Emberley. New York: Roaring Brook Press.

Emberley, Rebecca, and Ed Emberley. 2013. *Itsy Bitsy Spider*. Portsmouth, NH: Two Little Birds.

Ferry, Beth. 2015. *Stick and Stone*. Illustrated by Tom Lichtenheld. New York: HMH Books for Young Readers.

Fox, Mem. *Hattie and the Fox*. Illustrated by Patricia Mullins. New York: Simon & Schuster Books for Young Readers.

Franco, Betsy. 2007. *Birdsongs.* Illustrated by Steve Jenkins. New York: Margaret K. McElderry Books.

Fyleman, Rose. 2012. *Mice.* Illustrated by Lois Ehlert. New York: Beach Lane Books.

Gibbons, Gail. 1991. *From Seed to Plant.* New York: Holiday House.

Guy, Ginger Foglesong. 2007. *Fiesta!* Illustrated by Rene King Moreno. New York: Greenwillow Books.

Hale, Christy. 2012. *Dreaming Up: A Celebration of Building.* New York: Lee & Low Books.

Harrison, Hannah E. 2015. *Bernice Gets Carried Away.* New York: Dial Books.

Henkes, Kevin. 2009. *Birds.* Illustrated by Laura Dronzek. New York: Harper-Collins Children's Books.

Hoban, Tana. 1990. *Shadows and Reflections.* New York: Greenwillow Books.

———. 1999. *Let's Count.* New York: Greenwillow Books.

Hutchins, Pat. 1987. *Changes, Changes.* New York: Aladdin.

Ives, Penny. 2006. *Rabbit Pie.* Swindon, UK: Child's Play International.

———. 2007. *Five Little Ducks.* Swindon, UK: Child's Play International.

Jackson, K., and B. Jackson. 1975. *The Saggy Baggy Elephant.* Illustrated by Tenggren. New York: Golden Books.

Jenkins, Emily. 2005. *Five Creatures.* Illustrated by Tomek Bogacki. New York: Square Fish.

Kalman, Bobbie. 1997. *How a Plant Grows.* St. Catharine's, ON: Crabtree.

Klassen, Jon. 2012. *This Is Not My Hat.* Somerville, MA: Candlewick.

Krinitz, Esther Nisenthal, and Bernice Steinhardt. 2010. *Memories of Survival.* Illustrated by Esther Nisenthal Krinitz. Washington, DC: Art and Remembrance.

Lester, Helen. 1988. *Tacky the Penguin.* Illustrated by Lynn Munsinger. New York: Houghton Mifflin.

———. 2012. *All for Me and None for All.* Illustrated by Lynn Munsinger. New York: HMH Books for Young Readers.

Lionni, Leo. 1987. *Alexander and the Wind-Up Mouse.* New York: Dragonfly Books.

———. 1995. *Little Blue and Little Yellow.* New York: HarperCollins.

Litwin, Eric. 2012. *Pete the Cat and His Four Groovy Buttons.* Illustrated by James Dean. New York: HarperCollins.

Lowrey, Janette Sebring. 2001. *The Poky Little Puppy.* Illustrated by Gustaf Tenggren. New York: Golden Books.

Macaulay, David. 1998. *The New Way Things Work.* New York: HMH Books for Young Readers.

———. 2016. *The Way Things Work Now.* New York: HMH Books for Young Readers.

MacDonald, Margaret Read. 2005. *Fat Cat: A Danish Folktale.* Illustrated by Julie Paschkis. Little Rock, AK: August House LittleFolk.

Martin, Bill Jr. 1992. *Brown Bear, Brown Bear, What Do You See?* Illustrated by Eric Carle. New York: Henry Holt.

McCloskey, Robert. 1941. *Make Way for Ducklings.* New York: Viking.

Milne, A. A. 1996. *The Complete Tales and Poems of Winnie-the-Pooh.* Illustrated by Ernest H. Shepard. New York: Dutton Children's Books.

Moore, Lilian. 1995. "Construction." In *A Jar of Tiny Stars: Poems by NCTE Award-Winning Poets,* edited by Bernice E. Cullinan, 51. Honesdale, PA: Boyds Mills Press.

Mound, Laurence. 2007. *Eyewitness: Insect.* New York: DK Publishing.

Murphy, Stuart J. 2006. *Jack the Builder.* Illustrated by Michael Rex. New York: HarperCollins.

———. 2006b. *A Pair of Socks.* Illustrated by Lois Ehlert. New York: Harper Collins.

Nelson, Kadir. 2015. *If You Plant a Seed.* New York: Balzer + Bray.

Numeroff, Laura. 1985. *If You Give a Mouse a Cookie.* Illustrated by Felicia Bond. New York: HarperCollins.

Parr, Todd. 2005. *The Feelings Book.* New York: Little, Brown.

Paschkis, Julie. 2015. *P. Zonka Lays an Egg.* Atlanta: Peachtree.

Pinkney, Brian. 1997. *Max Found Two Sticks.* New York: Aladdin.

Pinkney, Jerry. 2006. *The Little Red Hen.* New York: Dial Books for Young Readers.

Prelutsky, Jack. 1986. *Read-Aloud Rhymes for the Very Young.* Illustrated by Marc Brown. New York: Alfred A. Knopf.

Prince, April Jones. 2006. *What Do Wheels Do All Day?* Illustrated by Giles Laroche. Boston: HMH Books for Young Readers.

Raschka, Chris. 2011. *A Ball for Daisy.* New York: Schwartz & Wade.

Rau, Dana Meachen. 1997. *A Box Can Be Many Things.* Illustrated by Paige Billin-Frye. Chicago: Children's Press.

Reynolds, Aaron. 2012. *Creepy Carrots.* Illustrated by Peter Brown. New York: Simon & Schuster Books for Young Readers.

Rohmann, Eric. 2007. *My Friend Rabbit.* New York: Square Fish.

Rosen, Michael. 1997. *We're Going on a Bear Hunt.* Illustrated by Helen Oxenbury. New York: Margaret K. McElderry Books.

Rosen, Michael, and Arthur Robins. 1993. *Little Rabbit Foo Foo.* New York: Aladdin.

Rosenthal, Amy Krouse. 2015. *Friendshape.* Illustrated by Tom Lichtenheld. New York: Scholastic.

Ruzzier, Sergio. 2015. *Two Mice.* New York: Clarion Books.

Salas, Laura Purdie. 2015. *A Rock Can Be. . . .* Illustrations by Violeta Dabija. Minneapolis: Millbrook.

Scarry, Richard. 1998. *Cars and Trucks and Things That Go.* New York: Golden Books.

Shannon, David. 1998. *No, David!* New York: Blue Sky Press.

———. 2002. *Duck on a Bike.* New York: Blue Sky Press.

Singer, Marilyn. 2012. *A Stick Is an Excellent Thing: Poems Celebrating Outdoor Play.* Illustrated by LeUyen Pham. New York: Clarion Books.

Stead, Philip C. 2010. *A Sick Day for Amos McGee.* Illustrated by Erin E. Stead. New York: Roaring Brook Press.

———. 2012. *Bear Has a Story to Tell.* Illustrated by Erin E. Stead. New York: Roaring Brook Press.

Stevenson, Robert Louis. 1999. "My Shadow." In *A Child's Garden of Verses* by Robert Louis Stevenson, edited by Tasha Tudor, 24. New York: Simon and Schuster Books for Young Readers.

Stojic, Manya. 2000. *Rain.* New York: Crown.

Symes, R. F. 2014. *Eyewitness: Rocks and Minerals.* New York: DK Publishing.

Swineburne, Stephen R. 2002. *Guess Whose Shadow?* Honesdale, PA: Boyds Mills Press.

Teague, David. 2015. *The Red Hat.* Illustrated by Antoinette Portis. New York: Disney-Hyperion.

Walsh, Ellen Stoll. 1991. *Mouse Count.* New York: Scholastic.

Willems, Mo. 2013. *A Big Guy Took My Ball!* New York: Disney-Hyperion.

Williams, Linda. 2002. *The Little Old Lady Who Was Not Afraid of Anything.* Illustrated by Megan Lloyd. New York: HarperCollins.

Wood, Audrey. 1984. *The Napping House.* Illustrated by Don Wood. San Diego: Harcourt.

Wood, Audrey, and Bruce Wood. 2004. *Ten Little Fish.* New York: Blue Sky Press.

Worth, Valerie. 1983. "Crickets." In *The Random House Book of Poetry for Children,* edited by Jack Prelutsky, 73. Illustrated by Arnold Lobel. New York: Random House.

Yaccarino, Dan. 2009. *Five Little Pumpkins.* New York: Scholastic.

Zelinsky, Paul O. 1990. *The Wheels on the Bus.* New York: Dutton Books for Young Readers.

Index